THE HIGH CROSSES OF IRELAND

THE HIGH CROSSES OF IRELAND

Inspirations in Stone

—▬—

Elinor D.U. Powell
with a foreword by Peter Harbison

The Liffey Press

Published by
The Liffey Press
Ashbrook House
10 Main Street, Raheny,
Dublin 5, Ireland
www.theliffeypress.com

A catalogue record of this book is
available from the British Library.

ISBN 978-1-905785-27-8

Editing and book design by Alicia McAuley.
Printed in Spain by Graficas Cems.

CONTENTS

ACKNOWLEDGEMENTS

I visited the sites pictured in this book over the years since childhood and spent many relaxing hours waiting for the sun to come around the vault of heaven to a particular angle and for the clouds to disperse. I then photographed the high crosses to be found at these sites and collected the results in a scrapbook. In published form, this would not have seen the light of day were it not for the kindness of many people.

The first person I want to acknowledge is my dear friend Erica Dodd, a noted authority on Christian and Islamic art of the eastern Mediterranean, who saw the photographs while on a visit to my home in Victoria, British Columbia. She coaxed me to show them to Dr Colum Hourihane, Director of the Index of Christian Art, Princeton University, on his visit to Victoria in the autumn of 2005. He was immediately impressed, said they comprised the best collection of colour photographs of the high crosses he had seen, and encouraged me to publish them. Dr Hourihane took the collection as it then stood and added it to the Index of Christian Art in the Department of Art and Archaeology at Princeton. Dr Dodd then spent countless hours reviewing my early drafts and coached me in how such a book should be put together. Speeding the collection along on its publication path was that notable authority on the high crosses of Ireland, Dr Peter Harbison, whose foreword graces this volume.

I would also like to thank my brother, Stephen Powell, of Birr, County Offaly, who was kind enough to drive me around Ireland in 2006 to take further pictures and complete the collection. Ireland is a small country, but we managed to cover many miles as we trekked back and forth. Finally, I would like to thank his wife, June, for preparing all those tasty lunches we enjoyed on the way.

ILLUSTRATIONS

Chapter 4

Chapter 6

Chapter 7

Chapter 8

Chapter 9

Foreword

Those great tall stone crosses standing out in Ireland's countryside are the country's greatest contribution to world sculpture, and contain the largest amount of religious carving preserved anywhere in Europe from the last quarter of the first Christian millennium. They are found in what are now churchyards but were once monasteries of piety and peace, which spread Ireland's zeal for learning and scholarship across the European continent. These crosses stand as elegant monuments to a high civilisation; their shape, with the characteristic ring around the cross's head, became such a potent nationalistic symbol in the mid-nineteenth century that it was used for grave memorials on both sides of the Atlantic for those who wanted to identify themselves as Irish.

The glory of this book is that it allows us to stand, figuratively, in front of these high crosses, to look in wonder at their varying shapes and sizes, and to admire the quality of master carvers' work of a thousand years ago. It does this through Elinor Powell's excellent illustrations – the fruit of two extensive photo sessions, one in 1989 and the other in 2006. The earlier group shows how chemical spraying around 1980 had largely rid the stone of lichens, whereas the later group shows these disfiguring growths reappearing – without, however, any damage having been done to the carving. Other than the occasional incident of local vandalism or the iconoclastic actions of seventeenth-century religious zealots, the main damage done to the crosses has been through acid rain and exposure to the Irish weather for a millennium and more. How crisp the original carving was can best be seen underneath the rings and arms of the crosses, where wind and rain have not encroached on the stone so much. Some few, at sites like Moone and Clonmacnoise, have been brought indoors by government authorities in order to preserve them for future generations. This, however, has the downside that the keen photographer is now prevented from taking pictures of these crosses in their original landscape setting, with the sun shining obliquely to bring out the light and shadow effects of their figure sculpture and ornamental patterns, as Dr Powell has managed to do so successfully.

This is a book essentially to help us enjoy the visual aspect of these crosses without overburdening us with long and tiresome text. The author gives us just the right amount of introductory matter, thereby allowing the eye to concentrate on the monuments themselves – which is as it ought to be. More than any other book I know, this volume brings out the dimensional depth of the crosses by showing many of them from a diagonal rather than from a frontal stance. But above all, it is the first time that so many of these beautiful crosses have been illustrated in *colour* between the covers of a single book.

It is wonderful to see how Dr Powell's childhood fascination for these monuments has kept her determined to bring this daunting project to fruition and to bring alive again, through her remarkable photographic skills and stamina, these pictorial Bibles in stone. I know all too well myself how long it takes to get the best coverage, waiting for that rare and magical moment when sun and cloud together combine to give the optimum effect. It has been a great pleasure for me to relive visits to these crosses through Dr Powell's admirable and often atmospheric pictures, and I hope that her sense of wonderment and delight will be communicated through them to what I hope will be the many readers of, and browsers through, this truly remarkable volume.

Dr Peter Harbison
Honorary Academic Editor, Royal Irish Academy

INTRODUCTION

The high crosses of Ireland are truly inspirational. In form and design they stand alone in the world. Some idea of their grandeur can be appreciated by photographs and I have been encouraged to make my personal collection available to a wider public. Other books and collections are available for further study, such as the comprehensive catalogue by Peter Harbison,[1] to which I will make frequent reference throughout this book, as well as a variety of monographs on specific sites.

The term 'high cross' is a puzzle to many people. It was first mentioned in the thousand-year-old *Annals of the Four Masters*.[2] Specialists are still not clear as to what should be included under the title, but it is usually meant to indicate a cross carved out of stone (or originally of wood), with a ring connecting the arms and shaft, embellished with figurative and decorative motifs. Found almost exclusively in Ireland and those parts of British Isles with connections to Celtic traditions, these crosses were erected at a time when monumental art had ceased to be built in other parts of Europe, owing to the chaos following the fall of the Roman Empire.

The building of the high crosses follows the time in history that saw the production of beautiful illuminated books such as the *Book of Kells* and the *Book of Durrow*. Many of these books were destroyed in the looting and burning carried out by Viking and other invaders in Ireland. The stone high crosses were more durable and, by being placed outside the small churches, were available to the illiterate countrymen who came to learn about the sacred stories they portrayed. How fortunate we are that the artists and their patrons turned to that less-destructible material, the rock of the land on which they stood. The ancient sculptors have left the record of their vision in monuments that have survived, in varying degrees of preservation, until the present time.

Forgotten for centuries by all but a few local inhabitants and some discerning antiquarians, the high crosses were discovered and brought to public attention less than 200 years ago, when George Petrie carried out a survey to record each site,[3] and Henry O'Neill published lithographs of the crosses of special interest to him.[4] Recently, interpretative centres have been established in important archeological sites to help both stranger and native appreciate these unique monuments of the past.

Ever since my parents took me as a child to visit sacred sites like Kells and Clonmacnoise, I have found myself drawn back from western Canada to stand in their presence, to reflect and to re-collect their images. Holidays have taken me to these sites over many years, and the photographs were taken in various forms – first in black and white, then in colour transparencies and finally in colour prints. Over the years change is evident also in the increasing interest shown by the Irish cultural authorities in the care and maintenance of these sites and their monuments. The greatest developments have been seen in the last 20 years, with the removal of some crosses to protect them from pollution and from vandalism. The photographs taken during my visit in 2006 show some of the most recent changes.

When I show these pictures to friends in Canada, they are introduced to a spiritually based art of which many were previously unaware. The accompanying text will tell the reader something of the context and background of the high crosses, as well as providing a verbal description.

1. Harbison, Peter, *The High Crosses of Ireland: An Iconographical and Photographic Survey* (Bonn: Dr Rudolf Habelt GMBH, 1992).
2. *Ibid.*
3. Petrie, George, *The Ecclesiastical Architecture of Ireland Anterior to the Norman Invasion* (Dublin: Hodges and Smith, 1845).
4. O'Neill, Henry, *Illustrations of the Most Interesting of the Sculptured Crosses of Ancient Ireland* (London: Trübner, 1857).

Chapter 1

Ireland and the Coming of Christianity

Geographical Background

In some ways Ireland seems remote, and that remoteness was instrumental in the happenstance that she was never invaded by the Romans. Yet other, more nautical, peoples of that time saw her as a link between northern and southern parts of western Europe, between the Iberian Peninsula and Scandinavia. There is even evidence of links between Ireland and places as far away as Asia, Egypt and north Africa (Fig. 1) in the form of art and religious practices.[1]

Fig. 1. Sources of influence on Irish Christian art.

Washed by the Gulf Stream, Ireland shares with her north European neighbours a mild climate, braced by the rains and winds of ocean storms. Mountains and hills of granite, as well as metamorphic rocks forged from volcanic action, gird the coastline. In discrete upland areas, sandstone deposited in ancient seas has come to the surface through geological upheaval and the weathering away of the overlying limestone strata. In the west, in County Clare, the Ice Age 10,000 years ago rubbed off the overlying soil, leaving an escarpment of exposed limestone.[2]

These rock formations provide the building materials for the high crosses photographed in this book. Their endurance against the ravages of our Irish weather depends on both the type and the quality of the stone chosen by their ancient masons. Most crosses are of sandstone, apparently chosen for it hardness, which derives from its grit and quartzite content. Some, composed of softer rock, show severe weathering with great loss of detail, while others, more durable, appear almost as perfect as the day they were carved.

THE ANCIENT PEOPLE OF IRELAND

The people who were to embrace the Christian gospel in the fifth century of the Common Era with such apparent avidity could trace their ancestry to the end of the last Ice Age, when succeeding waves of migrants came by sea from the continent of Europe and north Africa and settled in Ireland. They cleared the forests with stone axes and raised cattle, horses, sheep and goats. Using wooden ploughs at first and later, with the discovery of iron, metal ones, they tilled the land and grew wheat and barley.[3]

People travelled by boat along the coastline and on the rivers. Within Ireland the River Shannon formed one particularly important north–south passageway. On land, travel was more tedious and fraught with danger. In some places making one's way was facilitated by the presence of eskers – high elongated ridges left behind by the Ice Age. The most important esker extends from west to east across the country, providing dry ground above the lakes and bogs and through the forests. Tribespeople of the Neolithic period built megalithic monuments, such as that at Newgrange (Fig. 2 shows the decorated stone at the entrance) about 5,000 years ago.[4] These sites possess the first depiction of the intricate spiral incisions on carved stones that are so much in evidence on the high crosses erected 4,000 years later (Fig. 3).

About 500 years before the birth of Christ, the Iron Age brought new ideas, ideologies and values. Immigrants from the continent brought their art, their language and their way of life, blending in with the original inhabitants and adopting their culture. An elite plutocracy could foster the creation of gold and

Top: Fig. 2. Stone with spiral decoration at doorway of Newgrange.
Left and above: Fig. 3. Spirals on high crosses at Drumcliff and Ahenny.

other ornaments. A culture of heroic warriors developed; the sagas that have come down to us speak of continuing skirmishes and battles between tribes. Yet this is only part of the story. A sophisticated and complex system of laws developed, with its roots in ancient Indo-European custom rather than in Roman law.[5] There were druids and priests. The druids formed the learned class: they included teachers and philosophers, theologians, lawyers and judges. Their central moral philosophy was the soul's immortality and the notion of a day of judgement.[6] These basic beliefs may well have facilitated the reception of Christianity at the time of St Patrick and others, who introduced this religion in the fifth century.

Druids were responsible for passing on their wisdom to their apprentices, who studied for many years before becoming druids in their own right. Learning and the transmission of knowledge were entirely oral; we have found out about them mainly from the reports of Latin writers of the time and from other accounts written many years later. Priests were a separate order from the druids and were generally responsible for the actual rites of worship. The pre-Christian inhabitants of Ireland had their gods, representing various aspects of nature, worshipping in specially hallowed groves. Prominent and given high status were the poets, the musicians and the artists. Celtic art of great beauty is to be found on gold and bronze ornaments and on stone monuments. This Celtic art was to be retained and developed to a high art form in the Christian era, as we shall see.

Society also included farming folk, who raised the flocks and tilled the land. There were no towns or cities; instead, there were small settlements of extended family members living under the protection and control of a local king or chieftain. There were no coins in common usage, so trade was reciprocated in a number of other ways: by service, by obligation, in kind and by bartering.[7] Wealth was reckoned by the number of cattle a chieftain or farmer possessed.

It is evident that pre-Christian Celtic society was a complex one, with standards of honour and bravery, a people devoted to great learning and art and an infrastructure of farming and husbandry. Tribal warfare was common among the rival leaders, who formed the free elite. Below them were a number of different ranks, from the educated bards and druids to the tenant farmers and serfs.[8] While society appeared ready to accept the new vision that the great Christian missionaries and their followers were to bring, it had the internal strengths to preserve the essences of the old culture, to incorporate the new teachings into their understanding and to create a new and particular Irish identity. This identity was strong enough and isolated enough to hold back, at least for a time, the strictures of a more formal patriarchal organisation introduced by later invasions and church hierarchies.

Early Christianity in Ireland

The record of the introduction of Christianity is difficult to interpret because so many of the Celtic traditions of communication were oral, and their content was written down either much later or by foreign writers.[9] Christianity had come to some parts of Ireland even before St Patrick arrived in 432 CE to challenge and convert the old secular order at Tara's Hill. St Patrick introduced Latin and writing, leaving behind several important documents from his own hand. These include a set of canons or rules of ecclesiastical discipline and the famous 'St Patrick's Breastplate', translated as follows:

> I arise today,
> Through a mighty strength, the invocation of the Trinity,
> Through belief in the threeness,
> Through confession of the oneness,
> Of the Creator of Creation.[10]

St Patrick, who must have been a charismatic individual, appears to have converted many people to Christianity. His brand of Christianity appears to have been benign: he did not forbid any native practices that did not clash with the word of God. Christianity brought a new ethic, focused on caring relationships between people and on individual asceticism. It is remarkable how quickly Christianity spread through the land. However, the old ways of valorous warriors and their heroic deeds continued. The two ethical systems seem to have existed side by side, influencing each other.[11]

Independent of the episcopal organisation established by St Patrick, and soon to overwhelm it, was the development of monasteries.[12] The monastic founders, starting less than 20 years after St Patrick's death, appear to have looked not to St Patrick and Rome but to Britain and St Ninian for their organisational sources. Their model appears also to have come from the Desert Fathers' monastic hermitages of Egypt and Syria.[13] Familiar names include St Columba of Meath and Iona and St Ciaran of Clonmacnoise. These early saints were exceptional leaders, exhibiting a high level of commitment to the word of God and the gospel, and living lives that combined an asceticism and discipline with pastoral care toward others.[14]

The monasteries, originally intended as retreats from the world, places of asceticism and strict discipline, soon became influential and powerful establishments in the life of the country. They provided centres that combined many functions previously lacking: hostels for travellers, hospices for the sick, places of prayer and spiritual healing, reformatories and workshops for the production of artistic artefacts. Within their walls was a renewed focus on learning: this function was taken from the druidic system and developed. The religion of compassion, redemption and pastoral care brought new life, hope and joy to the local people.

Undergirding the monastic settlements were several contrasting theologies that show up in themes portrayed in the carvings on the high crosses. These theologies included the life-affirming teachings and practices of the earlier saints already mentioned. These saints also affirmed the indigenous culture's deep connection with nature. The sacred groves and wells of pagan times were rededicated to Christianity. St Columba is said to have reconsecrated over 300 well-springs.[15] The other potent stream of continuing influence was that of the Desert Fathers of Egypt. St Anthony and St Paul, who, as a response to the decadence that had engulfed secular Rome after its destruction by the Visigoths in 410 CE, retreated to a life of asceticism in the north African desert.[16] There they were joined by others, who came to share their practices and devotions. Out of these nuclei developed the disciplined monastic rules of their organisation. Time and time again this ascetic tradition provided checks against the growing affluence and secularisation of the monastic orders.

The period during which high crosses appeared extends from the seventh century through to the twelfth. Their erection occurred in three phases, separated by significant reform movements. The early Donegal crosses that remain are dated to the seventh century. The scriptural high crosses of the midlands and elsewhere were created in the ninth and tenth centuries. The final period of cross building is firmly placed by historians in the twelfth century, when they were constructed in relation to the setting up of a diocesan system similar to that of England and continental Europe, and under the control of the Vatican. Formally organised monastic orders from the continent, such as the Cistercians, were founded in Ireland at that time, and the unique indigenous artistic tradition represented by the high crosses ceased, at least for a while.[17]

Monastery Buildings

Almost all of the churches and other monastery buildings that existed during the time of the construction of the high crosses were of timber, and none of these structures has survived.[18] Later, small stone churches were built, often several together – the abbots appear to have opted for small buildings. These, in turn, have largely disappeared and the high crosses are now associated with larger church buildings of a later date, adorned by splendid doorways of Romanesque style. Contemporary with the main high crosses, and continuing into the twelfth century, are the round

Fig. 4. Schema of a monastic site (drawing by James Gardner).

towers, unique to Ireland, whose main function seems to have been to serve as belfries, storage depositories and watchtowers. Many of the high crosses are in close proximity to the round towers, such as those of Clonmacnoise and Monasterboice, while other crosses are to be found in association with post-Reformation Protestant parish churches.

Monasteries grew in size and influence: some, such as that at Clonmacnoise, became great ecclesiastical centres with many buildings and churches (Fig. 4). These centres took on the characteristics of towns and had the resources to create workshops for the production of beautiful reliquaries, shrines and other metalwork.[19] Writing was undertaken in both Latin and Irish. Skilled craftsmen of an order seldom rivalled either before or since developed a rich and varied literature and artistic culture. Copyists spent many hours transcribing sacred texts and developing the art of illumination that is so characteristic of this period of Irish Christianity. When foreign invaders from Scandinavia started to destroy these books and reliquaries, the monasteries turned to erecting more durable monuments to get their message out to the faithful: the high crosses became their Bibles in stone. The scriptural high crosses, which are the most remarkable and unique, were built at a time when Viking raids and internal contention made for instability throughout the countryside.

THE HIGH CROSSES

The high crosses that have survived are all carved from rock. They were probably preceded by wooden crosses for use in processions and as standing monuments.

The Vikings started their raids in the eighth century and continued for 300 years. At first these raids were sporadic.[20] Later, large fleets entered the major rivers, including the Shannon and the Boyne. The raiders pillaged and destroyed the monasteries and their priceless artefacts and killed the monks and lay people within them. It was in this time of great duress that the monasteries turned to stone as a more enduring means of conveying the Christian message.

The ninth and tenth centuries were also a time of reform, when leaders in centres near what is now Dublin became distressed about the laxity, disorganisation, secularisation and corruption that had become the norm in many monasteries. St Maelruin of Tallaght and Finglas near Dublin brought in a reform movement known as Céli Dé, which provided a system for the return of asceticism, discipline and adherence to a devotional life. According to Lord Killalin and Michael Duignan, 'This movement of reform was of great significance for art and literature, and has left as its memorial the great figured high crosses of the 9th and 10th centuries.'[21] The Irish monasteries still remained autonomous and independent of one another, however, subject to the authority of their leader[22] and often closely connected by family to the secular ruler of the tribe or kingdom.

It was in the context of these turbulent times that the scriptural high crosses were erected. But what do these crosses signify? They are unique in a number of ways. Firstly, they have a very distinctive shape. A typical outline is provided here, although there was much variation, as will be seen. Most characteristic of the Celtic high crosses is the presence of a ring connecting the arms, head and shaft. Also to be noted is the scalloping of the crosses' main arms, which provides complementary curves to the arcs of the rings. Often within the spaces between arc and cross are small cylinders or volutes. These may be attached to the arc or to the cross itself. The shaft is raised on a base, sometimes with a plinth between these two parts.

The meaning of the ring has remained a subject for conjecture. Some hold that it is a sign of the sun, or of eternity.[22] Others suggest an alternative to the customary meaning of the cross of which it forms a part.[23] We have come to see the cross as a symbol of the crucifixion of Jesus Christ. Bryce (1989) and Richardson and Scarry (1990) suggest that it is derived from another, earlier, symbol of Christianity: the chi-rho monogram. These letters are the first two in the Greek name of Christ. The monogram was common in many forms of Christian art in the Mediterranean as early as the fourth century, and is found in the *Book of Kells* and some grave slabs. The ring as portrayed on the high crosses has been used in paintings as a nimbus or halo behind the head of Christ and the saints. It has also been used to depict the sun. 'As a solar symbol it has a lot to do with the representation of Christ in

Majesty, Divine Light; it being understood that the early Christians never looked at it in any terms other than this,' acknowledges Bryce. The presence of a halo points surely to the sacredness of the stories behind all the figures and designs depicted on the crosses. These symbols may act as mediators of deep faith to those who contemplate their message. Many viewers of these high crosses, even today, become aware of an aura about them which persists despite weathering, their damaged state and recently, their relocation to places of greater safety.

Figure 5 shows a 'typical' cross, with its component parts identified. It is representative of those carved in the ninth and tenth centuries.

Additional to the shape of the crosses is their unique decoration with intricate interwoven patterns, which have more to do with the old Irish art forms and mythic tales than with Christianity. They developed from those Celtic cultural streams

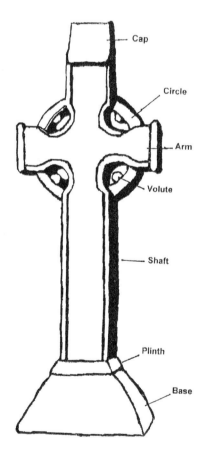

Fig. 5. Outline of ninth–tenth-century high cross, with parts identified.

in Ireland predating Christianity and continued for hundreds of years after the introduction of that religion. The imagination of the scribes, coming from a culture imbued with a profound belief in the mystical and the notion that animals could change their shapes and undergo transformation, found free rein in the illumination of sacred texts and high crosses alike. Human and animal heads appear at the corners of areas of interlacing; serpents form entangled patterns. Spirals, interlacing patterns and a wide variety of fret patterns and diagonals are to be seen on the crosses, sometimes in separate panels, sometimes free-ranging along the surface. Even the faces of the rings are covered by an ever-varying pattern of interlacing.

In the context of these decorative patterns, the scriptural crosses introduced new elements that the illuminated books had not covered: graphic depictions of the stories of the Old and New Testaments. Certain themes predominate. The crucifixion is often seen on one side of a cross, with Christ in glory on the other. A common depiction of Christ's ministry is the miracle of the feeding of the 5,000. But Christianity arose out of a long chapter of Jewish history and tradition and the story of Adam and Eve, of Cain and Abel and of Isaac's near-sacrifice at the hands of his father are common themes also. As exemplified by these crosses, Celtic Christianity is pre-eminent in combining Christian and non-Christian themes in its portrayal of sacred objects.

It appears that high crosses always stood outside the small churches but within the monastery walls. Thus they served several purposes. They could be used as teaching devices – pictorial Bibles in stone, as it were – for the education of the illiterate local

Fig. 6. North Cross, Castledermot: illustration by Francis Grose compared to modern photograph.

community. They became places of pilgrimage and were often located at the edge of monastery grounds to mark their boundaries. Moreover, as noted earlier, they could not easily be damaged or carried away. Many more perishable items such as reliquaries and illuminated books were destroyed or looted in the troubled times of invasion and internal conflict during the ninth and tenth centuries.

The scribes' inspiration did not continue indefinitely: as noted, the eleventh century was devoid of further high-cross carving. In the twelfth century the crosses were associated with the recently revived dioceses rather than any monastic orders. The crosses merely show figures of crucifixions or of bishops along with the Celtic designs. After the arrival of the Norman invaders towards the end of the twelfth century, no further high crosses were erected. Strangely, it was then that the Romanesque churches with their beautiful carved archways were built, providing a background to the earlier crosses.

How well have these monuments withstood the centuries that have elapsed since they were erected? History's sword has been double edged. Outright destruction and pillage came in the form of Viking raiders, who burnt and looted consecrated buildings: for example, Clonmacnoise was plundered and burned dozens of times between the ninth and thirteenth centuries. Later, Henry VIII and his descendants disestablished the monasteries and the buildings fell into ruin, their lands confiscated and transferred to English settlers. With the development of the Reformation and its spread to Ireland, Protestant parishes took over many of the old monastic sites and parish churches were built sporadically over the ensuing centuries. The crosses became part of the landscape, largely neglected. It was not until the end of the eighteenth century that an interest in the ecclesiastical architecture of Ireland began. However, most of the descriptions written concentrated on the round towers and medieval churches. High crosses, when mentioned at all, were seen as crude, debased and in ruin, or else romanticised. For instance, Francis Grose,[24] writing at the end of the eighteenth century, had as his title page the head of a high cross snapped off from its shaft. If this was a depiction of the North Cross at Castledermot, as seems likely, that cross was in fact (and is still) intact at the junction of head with shaft, although the bottom of the shaft does display a break in continuity with its base (Fig. 6). Some illustrations from the middle of the nineteenth century appear overly romantic, with the round towers covered in ivy and peasants kneeling before a cross at an appealing angle, such as Bartlett's depiction of a scene at Clonmacnoise in 1842 (Fig. 7).[25] However, it appears that the Cross of the Scriptures was indeed at a dangerous angle, as confirmed by one of the earliest photographs of that site, taken not long afterwards (Fig. 8).

Henry O'Neill published a collection of lithographs of many of the high crosses in 1857.[26] In later chapters of this book we will have an opportunity to compare his depictions with photographs taken 150 years later, over the last 20 years. With the

Above: Fig. 7. Bartlett's view of Clonmacnoise. *Right:* Fig. 8. Photograph taken in 1860s (Stereo Collection, National Library of Ireland).

Fig. 9. Repair of the cross at Moone as of 1989 and recent restoration.

publicity given to O'Neill's lithographs, and following the Industrial Exhibition in Dublin in 1853 (when ancient Irish material, including actual examples of the high crosses, was exhibited),[27] ringed crosses became popular – not for proclaiming the stories of sacred scripture as they had done 800 years previously, but as headstones for graves.

The history of the high crosses continues. Fragments have been collected and put together, though not always with the parts they had originally belonged to. Some have been collected and placed in areas other than those in which they were first erected. Recently some have been removed for safety from unprotected sites. For instance, in 1989, when many of the photos in this album were taken, the Market Cross stood in the middle of the bustling town of Kells. After being hit by a bus, it was re-erected in a clear space at the end of the town. The Cross of the Scriptures and other high crosses at Clonmacnoise have been placed inside the nearby Interpretative Centre, while replicas stand in the original site. Some fragments still remain unincorporated, such as two beautiful fragments left behind a mausoleum at Cashel, photographed in 2005. Other monuments have undergone restoration, such as that at Moone, County Kildare, where one can see how the old, crude repair has been replaced by a careful matching of the granite (Fig. 9).

The illustrations shown here are by no means exhaustive. For a more extensive record, with documentation, the reader should consult Peter Harbison's 1992 comprehensive analysis and catalogue.[28] Yet even that book is no longer complete.

13

Pl. 1. Two fragments of cross heads lying in the churchyard at Cashel.

New high crosses are still being discovered, such as the eight mini-high crosses in Nobber, County Meath, which appeared in 2005 when the churchyard ivy was trimmed.[29] And even in that centre of intense archeological interest, the Rock of Cashel, fragments of a high-cross head were found as late as 2005 (Pl. 1).

The plan here is to present the high crosses in roughly chronological order, as far as is possible to determine at present, in order to trace their beginning, their flowering, and eventual decline (Fig. 10). This approach will stretch from the very north of the country, close to Malin Head, to the fertile fields in the centre of Ireland. Here high crosses of a wide variety are to be found, including the glorious scriptural crosses. The survey will then travel south-west to the ancient flat limestone flags of County Clare, where the tale comes to an end as the inspiration for figurative art declines and fades away.

The photographs were taken mostly in 1989 and 1990, when many of the high crosses were in more natural surroundings than their present locations within old church ruins or interpretative centres. Thus these somewhat older photographs portray a context of the situation of the high crosses in sacred places from long ago, which is no longer the case. Preservation and, in some cases, restoration have necessarily taken priority over setting. Those more scenic photographs taken in 1989, therefore, reflect a reality that is no more: settings that enhanced the experience to be gained from contemplating these sacred emblems of the Christian faith. Further photographs were taken in 2006 and these document the changes that have occurred in order to enable this precious inheritance to be protected.

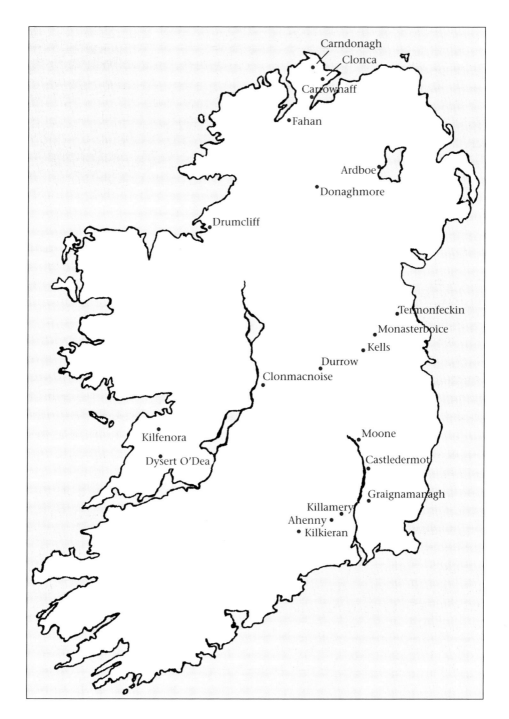

Fig. 10. Sites of high crosses included in this book.

1. Mitchell, Frank, 'Foreign Influences and the Beginnings of Irish Art', in Various authors, *Treasures of Irish Art 1500 BC to 1500 AD* (New York: Metropolitan Museum of Art, 1997), p. 57; Quinn, Bob, *The Atlantean Irish: Ireland's Oriental and Maritime Heritage* (Dublin: Lilliput Press, 2005).

2. Mitchell, Frank. *Reading the Irish Landscape* (Dublin: Wild Irish Library, 1976), p. 97.

3. Feehan, John, *Farming in Ireland: History, Heritage and Environment* (University of Dublin, 2003), p. 53.

4. O'Kelly, Michael J., *Newgrange: Archaeology, Art and Legend* (London: Thames and Hudson, 1982), p. 22.

5. McGrath, Fergal, *Education in Ancient and Medieval Ireland* (Dublin: Skellig Press, 1979), p. 17.

6. Olden, Thomas, *The Church of Ireland* (London: Wells Gardner, Darton & Co., 1892), p. 3.

7. Feehan *op. cit.*, p. 57.

8. *Ibid.*, p. 63.

9. Richter, Michael, *The Formation of the Medieval West* (Dublin: Four Courts Press, 1994), p. 81.

10. Translated by Kuno Meyer in Brendan Kennelly (ed.), *The Penguin Book of Irish Verse* (London: Penguin, 1970), p. 45.

11. Richter *op. cit.*, p. 183.

12. Hughes, Kathleen and Hamlin, Ann, *Celtic Monasticism: The Modern Traveller to the Early Irish Church* (New York: Seabury Press, 1981), p. 7.

13. de Paor, Liam, 'The Christian Triumph: The Golden Age' in Various authors *op. cit.*, p. 93; Harbison, Peter, *The Golden Age of Irish Art: The Medieval Achievement 600–1200* (London: Thames and Hudson, 1999), p. 27.

14. Bradley, Ian, *Celtic Christian Communities* (Kelowna: Northstone, 2000), p. 8.

15. Feehan *op. cit.*, p. 485.

16. Olden *op. cit.*, p. 71; Anson, Peter F., *The Call of the Desert: The Solitary Life in the Christian Church* (London: S.P.C.K., 1964), p. 54.

17. Carville, Geraldine, *The Occupation of Celtic sites in Medieval Ireland by the Canons Regular of St Augustine and the Cistercians* (Cistercian Studies Series no. 56) (Kalamazoo: Cistercian Publications, 1982), p. 14.

18. Leask, Harold, *Irish Churches and Monastic Buildings* (vol. i, Dundalk: Dundalgan Press, 1955), p. 5.

19. There are many books describing the metalwork and illuminated books of the early Christians, notably: Scherman, Katharine, *The Flowering of Ireland* (London: Little, Brown, 1981) p. 230; Harbison 1999 *op. cit.*, Lucas, A.T., *Treasures of Ireland* (Dublin: Viking Press, 1973); Various authors *op. cit.*.

20. Henry, Françoise, *Irish Art during the Viking Invasion 800–1020 AD* (London: Methuen, 1967), p. 8.

21. Killanin, Lord and Duignan, Michael V., *Shell Guide to Ireland* (London: Ebury Press, 1962), p. 20.

22. Carville *op. cit.*, p. 5.

23. Bryce, Derek, *Symbolism of the Celtic Cross* (Llanerch Enterprises, 1989), p. 33; Richardson, H. and Scarry, J., *An Introduction to Irish High Crosses* (Dublin: Mercier Press, 1990), p. 11.

24. Grose, Francis, *The Antiquities of Ireland* (vol. ii, London: M. Hooper, 1795), frontispiece.

25. Bartlett, H., contrib. to N.P. Willis, *The Scenery and Antiquities of Ireland* (London: G. Virtue, 1842).

26. Scarry, John, 'Early Photographs of Clonmacnoise' in Heather A. King (ed.), *Clonmacnoise Studies* (vol. i, Dublin: Dúchas, The Heritage Service, 1998), p. 19.

27. O'Neill, Henry, *Illustrations of the Most Interesting of the Sculptured Crosses of Ancient Ireland* (London: Trübner, 1857).

28. Williams, M. McE. 'Construction of the Market Cross at Tuam' in Colum Hourihane (ed.), *From Ireland Coming: Irish Art from the Early Christian to the Late Gothic Period in its European Context* (Princeton University Press, 2001).

29. Harbison, Peter, *The High Crosses of Ireland: An Iconographical and Photographic Survey* (vols i–iii, Bonn: Dr Rudolf Habelt GMBH, 1992).

30. Keogh, Elaine, 'Eight High Crosses Found in Co. Meath Village' in *Irish Times* (1 November 2005).

CHAPTER 2

EARLY CELTIC CROSSES IN COUNTY DONEGAL

The earliest Celtic crosses that still survive were erected in Ireland's most northerly county, Donegal. This may seem an isolated part of the island, and the Christian stone monuments are indeed separated by style, geography and date from those in other parts of Ireland. In those long-ago days, transport by water was often easier than transport by land. In its proximity to the rest of Ulster across the deep inlet of Lough Foyle, and to Scotland and even Scandinavia by the ocean route, the early Christians were quite well connected to offshore regions. The peninsula of Inishowen is the site of several of the earliest high crosses, dating back to the seventh century.[1] They were on the sites of early monasteries, which at that time were flourishing in Ireland.

While these early monasteries have since disappeared, art in the form of stone crosses or pillars has survived the centuries. Most had not yet developed to a form that we recognise as high crosses, being only vaguely cruciform, with no free ring. They are notable because of the blend of scriptural art and the Celtic designs already part of the culture to which Christianity brought its sacred message.

Far left: Pl. 2. Fahan Mura: east face. *Left:* Pl. 3. Fahan Mura: west face.

FAHAN MURA

The eighth-century pillar cross of Fahan Mura (Pl. 2), at the southern end of the Inishowen Peninsula, stands in the grounds of a monastery founded by St Columba in the sixth century. St Mura[2] was its first abbot. It is solid, with shallow lateral projections. Inscribed on both sides is a flat cross with expanded ends, filled with broad-ribbon interlacing.

Each face, while symmetrical in its own design, is of a different pattern from the other. We can note that the cruciform pattern is simpler on the east face than the west. On the east face the interlacing on the cross arms is almost straight edged, while on the west (Pl. 3) the edges of the inscribed cross are curved, with their expanded ends nearly meeting. Small medallions with concentric circles lie between the arms on the east side, oval bosses on the west. Two figures in profile oppose each other on the west face. They are shallowly inscribed, in contrast to the higher relief of the crosses. The statue combines a powerful emblem of Christianity with the labyrinthine curves of Celtic art, which invite contemplation and evoke a sense of the eternal. Men are portrayed, in contrast, as shallow and ephemeral. The cross thus represents a harmonious blend of two very different symbolic art forms. On the one

Right: Pl. 4. Carndonagh cross and pillars: east face.
Above: Fig. 11. Carndonagh: sketch of figures on shaft.

hand is the cross, central emblem of Christianity since the time of Constantine in the fourth century, which was accepted as a key to the understanding of that religion as the gospel story spread across Europe. The cruciform space is filled with the metaphors of eternity derived from pre-Christian Celtic art.

Evidence of the international connections and the educational sophistication of the monks and their craftsmen is to be found on the northern edge of the cross slab, where an inscription is written in Greek. Now indecipherable, earlier authorities[3] have noted that it read:

ΔΟΞΑ ΚΑΙ ΤΙΜΕ ΠΑΤΡΙ ΚΑΙ ΥΙΩ ΚΑΙ ΠΝΕΥΜΑΤΙ ΑΓΙΩ
Glory and honour to the father, son and holy spirit.

This is one of the few crosses that remain neglected by those interested in the preservation of our ancient monuments. Increasingly overgrown with long grasses and weeds, it stands in the vicinity of a crumbling ancient church whose walls are tumbling down with the weight of the ever-abundant ivy. By contrast, across the road is a newer parish church with an immaculate churchyard and well-kept graves.

Pl. 5. Carndonagh cross and pillars: west face.

CARNDONAGH AND CLONCA

Almost at the tip of the Inishowen Peninsula are the crosses of Carndonagh and Clonca. They are very different in style.

Pl. 6. Carndonagh: south and west aspects.

Pl. 7: Carndonagh, north pillar: west face, showing David playing the harp.

Pl. 8. Carndonagh, north pillar: south face, showing saucer-shaped decoration.

Carndonagh

As was the case at Fahan Mura, it is likely that there was a monastery at Carndonagh. The cross is associated with two smaller pillars. They were in the open air when the group pictures shown here were taken in 1989. They had already by then been moved a short distance from their original placing, and now they have been moved once more and placed under a wooden roof.

The side arms of the cross are very short and blunted. On the east-face shaft, well down from the head, which is filled with interlacing, is a low-relief picture of Christ with outstretched arms – as if on a crucifix, or possibly as if extending his arms to embrace mankind. The Christ image is set in the midst of five human figures in profile, two on each side of it and three below (Pl. 4).

Two pillars stand on each side of the cross. On the west side of the northern one is a picture of David playing his harp (Pl. 7). The south side of this pillar is deeply inscribed with three unequally sized double-spiral linked decorations (Pl. 8). A number of animal and human figures are inscribed on the southern pillar (see Pls 5, 6 and 9). The date of the Carndonagh cross and pillars is a matter of some debate. Hughes and Hamlin date them to the seventh century,[4] while Harbison[5] dates them to the eighth century or even the ninth.

Pl. 9. Carndonagh, south pillar:
unidentified figure.

Clonca

A standing cross at Clonca, close to Carndonagh, of uncertain date, has had most of its head replaced by smooth concrete. It has a tall shaft and short arms and, despite the repair work done, one can see the vestige of a circle on the top of the shaft and south arm, most visible on the west face (Pl. 11). The idea of a ring embracing the arms appears to have been emerging in the art of the sculptors around the time of this cross's construction.

The cross is of interest for several reasons. Firstly, it carries two examples of figurative art. On the top of the shaft on the east face is a panel depicting the feeding of the 5,000 with loaves and fishes (Pls 10 and 12). On the west face the image is in the centre of the elongated cross shaft, with interlacing above and below. Here are two seated figures who face us, portraying St Paul and St Anthony in the

Left: Pl. 10. Clonca: east face.
Below: Pl. 11. Clonca: west face, with ruined church.

Right: Pl. 12.
Clonca: shaft,
east face,
showing feeding
of the 5,000
and upper-panel
interlacing.
Far right: Pl. 13.
Clonca: west
face, showing
St Paul and St
Anthony in the
desert.

Right: Pl. 14.
Clonca: mid-
panel, east face,
showing zig-zag
patterning.
Far right: Pl. 15.
Clonca: east
face, showing
lower-panel
spirals.

desert (Pl. 13). Above them are two lion-like creatures in profile, who, the ancient story tells, came to the assistance of St Anthony. Of singular beauty are the areas of interlacing and other decorations that occupy the remainder of the east and west faces. These are worth examining. On the east side the upper panel consists of continuous carved ribbons tightly packed into the sides and corners of the enclosing

Pl. 16. Clonca: west face, comparing upper and lower panels.

panel, interwoven as they cross the panel eight times in each direction diagonally from side to side (Pl. 12). In the centre panel is a zigzag irregular pattern of moulded ridges (Pl. 14). The lower panel has quite a different design, with two loose spirals contained within the border (Pl. 15). The spirals are orientated in reverse to one another and their ends are expanded as they touch each other. Each seems to draw the eye into its centre, alternately, yet can be seen as a composite whole. On the west face, the interlacing is situated above and below the figures (Pl. 16), where the two panels can be contrasted. The pattern on the lower panel of the west face is coarser and contains fewer units than that of the upper panel.

Note can be made of the figurative art in this early Donegal series. While the Fahan Mura cross has no figures on it, on the Carndonagh cross the crucifixion is the dominant scene. In addition, there is a picture of David playing his harp from the Old Testament. This ancient instrument has been known across European civilisation from prehistoric times, and the Celtic harp has been popular in Irish history since the early Christian era, if not since before then. Perhaps the sculptors felt a special affinity with David the musician. From the New Testament is pictured the feeding of the 5,000: a story that exemplifies the epitome of hospitality and care for the crowds who came to hear Christ's teaching. Then, from the early post-scriptural period, we get a picture of the ascetic movement and the hermit withdrawn from society to the Egyptian desert, where St Paul and St Anthony found assistance from that most fearsome of wild beasts, the lion. While Irish writers on the early saints were famed for their portrayal in hagiographic style of signs and wonders too marvellous to be believed literally (such as the story of the life of St Columba as told by St Adamnan),[6] the practice of retreat from the world to the desert continued to be a powerful influence in monastic life during this period. The choice of these motifs as early priorities in portraying Bible stories appears revealing, but we must remember that the crosses of this period are the survivors of perhaps many more that are no longer in existence, and these may have highlighted other themes.

CARROWNAFF

This cross, standing at the edge of the road without decoration of any sort, lies close to Lough Foyle and is remarkable for its form, which seems to presage the development of the high cross in later centuries. It is otherwise quite plain and unremarkable. It introduces the new form of the cross, with the inner angles of the cross scalloped and the ring already present.

Pl. 17. Carrownaff: wayside cross.

1. Harbison, Peter, *The Golden Age of Irish Art: The Medieval Achievement 600–1200* (London: Thames and Hudson, 1999), p. 41.
2. Harbison, Peter, *Guide to National and Historic Monuments of Ireland* (3rd ed., Dublin: Gill and Macmillan, 2001), p. 100.
3. Harbison 1999 *op. cit.*, p. 51.
4. Hughes, Kathleen and Hamlin, Ann, *Celtic Monasticism: The Modern Traveller to the Early Irish Church* (New York: Seabury Press, 1981), p. 91.
5. Harbison 2001 *op. cit.*, p. 96.
6. Adamnan, St, *The Life of Saint Columba 521–597*, W. Huyshe, tr. (London: Routledge, 1905).

CHAPTER 3

THE GRANITE CROSSES OF THE BARROW VALLEY

This survey now drops south from the headlands of Donegal to the western edge of an ancient massive outcropping of granite. This extends in a wide strip south-westerly from the Irish Sea at Dublin Bay, under the Dublin and Wicklow Mountains to the southern end of the Barrow Valley. It is from this unlikely, uncompromising volcanic rock (unlikely because of its coarseness and irregularity as well as its hardness) that the early-Christian stonemasons first carved out the cross-and-ring form that they would develop to such a high level of artistry in the years to come. Granite is difficult to carve finely with the tools available during the period of construction, believed to be the early ninth century.

The sites at Castledermot and Moone, and further south at Graignamanagh, all lie on the westerly extension of the granite massif as it forms the easterly slope of the Barrow Valley. Numerous granite quarries are to be found in the area. The granularity of the stone used in the crosses, in its present weathered state, can be seen in a close-up of the base of the North Cross at Castledermot (Pl. 18). The granite crosses all lie within the Barrow Valley, with Graignamanagh a considerable distance to the south of the other two.

Pl. 18.
Castledermot
a small bee
highlights the
coarseness of
the granite.

Pl. 19. Graignamanagh: east faces of crosses (North Cross nearest camera).

Much research has been devoted to dating these high crosses and the experts are not sure about the sequence of their development. The earliest may be those at Graignamanagh, and the unusually proportioned cross at Moone may date to the very end of the eighth century.[1] The Castledermot crosses appear to be later, perhaps from the ninth century or even later, contemporary with the great scriptural crosses of the midlands.

GRAIGNAMANAGH, COUNTY KILKENNY

The two high crosses at Graignamanagh are within the churchyard of Duiske Cistercian Abbey, founded in the early thirteenth century. The crosses did not originate here, but were brought from elsewhere, from Ballogan (the North Cross) and from Aghailta.[2] They are not very tall, measuring less than two metres in height. The heads are solid, since the portions of the rings between the arms were not cut out. The rings on both crosses are marked off from the arms by indentations, which can be seen from either side but do not go all the way through, as is the case with the later crosses. The rings come to the edge of each arm. The arms are short, showing only a small degree of scalloping where they join, unlike later high crosses. Overall, they appear chunky and undeveloped, but are important in indicating an intermediate stage in evolution. The North Cross has a more decorated base and more slender proportions than the South Cross, but both are crude in their workmanship compared to others that lie further up the valley. Both crosses are seen in Plates 19 and 21.

Pl. 20. Graignamanagh: biblical scenes on North Cross.

North Cross

This cross has lost part of the shaft. In the lowest panel of the east face we can see that the figure of David is cut off at knee height.

East Face

On the east face (Pl. 19), the head is completely occupied by the crucifixion, with a smaller-scale soldier on each side of the central figure of Christ. Two oblong figures above may represent angels. To put the figures in chronological order as they appear in the Old Testament, the shaft can be read from the top down. It depicts first Adam and Eve beneath the tree of knowledge. The middle panel displays the sacrifice of Isaac, with Abraham standing on the right and Isaac in the centre, leaning back over the altar. The ram can be seen at the top left-hand corner. The lowest shaft panel shows David playing his harp. These themes are the most frequently repeated on many of the scriptural high crosses and we have already seen a version of David as a harpist in the Carndonagh pedestal.

Pl. 21. Graignamanagh: west faces of crosses
(South Cross nearest camera).

Pl. 22. Graignamanagh: west and south faces of North Cross, showing spiral interlacing and C-scrolls.

The base is in two sections, with an angular fret pattern in the upper part, and interlacing below. Much damage and repair are evident.

West Face

On the west face (Pl. 21), at the very top of the cross are two figures, dimly discernible. The scene can be identified as the Annunciation. The Angel Gabriel is shown on the left and the Virgin Mary is seated on the right. Except for a panel on the base of the shaft, the rest of this face is covered by a coarse network of interconnected spirals. The panel at the bottom of the shaft is almost indecipherable, but it may represent Mary greeting Elizabeth (Pl. 22).

North and South Sides

The shaft on the north side is decorated with an irregular fret pattern, now difficult to make out. The south-side shaft has a panel of interlocking angular C-scrolls (Pl. 22).

Base
The base on all sides suggests knots of interlacing, but is much worn.

South Cross
The base is modern, the north and south sides being plain.

East Face
The head shows the crucifix (Pl. 19). There is a fragment of interlacing at the top showing some damage, and there is some damage on the two arms. The shaft is covered by two panels of interlacing.

West Face
This face, like the east face, shows the crucifix, but the image is more indistinct (Pl. 21). The shaft is completely worn. Details of the north and south sides can no longer be made out.

All in all, the Graignamanagh crosses, though they appear unsophisticated and though they have been damaged over the years since their making, do show characteristics that were to be developed into a high art form within the next couple of hundred years.

MOONE, COUNTY KILDARE
The site is that of an early Columban monastery founded in the sixth century. The cross is believed to date from around 800 CE. It is thus from the same time as that at Graignamanagh, but very different in design and sophistication.

This high cross is like no other carved either before or after it. In contrast to the other granite crosses in the Barrow Valley, the sculptor adapted his design towards a stylised rendering of his themes, presenting the figures for the most part as flattened, rather than the more lifelike rounded ones seen elsewhere. The result is surely a powerful evocation of the stories they portray. The cross is also unusual in that the base is tall, about the same height as the shaft, and is shaped like a pyramid – narrower at the top – so that there is no step between shaft and base. The shaft is particularly narrow. There is a relatively small ring and biblical scenes, both Old and New Testament, are depicted on the base. The space between the ring and arms is cut away.

The cross used to stand to the south of the ruined church, and most of the pictures were taken in this position. It has now been moved by the Office of Public

Pl. 23. Moone: east face in graveyard (1989 photograph).

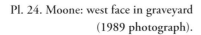
Pl. 24. Moone: west face in graveyard (1989 photograph).

Pl. 25. Moone: south side and east face (1989 photograph).

Works to within the ruins of the church, for safety. The pictures include those taken in 1989 in the grounds of the churchyard and some taken in 2006 at the cross's present site. A glass roof now protects it from the elements.

This is not the only change the cross has undergone in the last two centuries. In the 1857 lithographs of Henry O'Neill it appears much shorter (Figs 12 and 13). At the end of the nineteenth century, the shaft with its wondrous beasts was found in the churchyard. This piece was then inserted between the head and the base by Lord Walter Fitzgerald.[3] Thus it regained its stature. It now measures 7.65 metres in height and is in three parts: head, shaft and base. Since the cross was moved, the repair carried out earlier has been redone, with greater skill and with slightly paler granite.

The sections missing from the O'Neill lithographs can be seen in Plates 23 (east face), 24 and 26 (west face) and 25 (south side) and, in more detail, in Plates 27 (west face) and 28 (north side).

Pl. 26. Moone: west face
inside ruined church
(1989 photograph).

East Face

The figure of Christ in glory occupies the centre of the head. It has been deeply eroded over the years and only the dimmest outline can be made out. The shaft is covered by a number of panels with spiral and abstract designs (Pl. 23).

West Face

A spiral from which animal heads emerge decorates the centre of the cross. On the arms on each side are single human figures (Pl. 24).

Base

We can turn now to the more illustrative base and read in the chronological sequence of the Old Testament from the top down (and from right to left of the illustrations). On the east face are salient stories of the Old Testament: a graphic picture of Adam and Eve is enclosed within the confines of the narrowest, sloping part of the base (Pl. 29). Below them is the sacrifice of Isaac (Pl. 30) and below this a depiction of Daniel contending with seven lions – three on the left and four on the right (Pl. 31).

The stories thus portray the original sin of humankind, then two instances of God's saving grace. On the west face, the crucifixion occupies the narrow top of the base (Pl. 32). Underneath this are the 12 apostles, set side by side in three rows of four (Pl. 33). The base's north side features pictures of the desert hermits St Paul and St Anthony (Pl. 34). They break bread in the top panel. In the centre (Pl. 35), St Anthony is being tempted by two strange creatures with goat-like heads. A strange but beautiful six-legged creature occupies the lowest panel (Pl. 36). This latter figure seems to come straight out of pre-Christian, Celtic, mythology.

South Side

The south side includes one scene from the Old Testament, namely the three children in the fiery furnace (Pl. 37). Below them is a unique nativity scene: the flight of the holy family into Egypt to escape Herod's attempt to destroy the infant Jesus (Pl. 38).

Below: **Fig. 12. O'Neill lithograph of Moone High Cross (Special Collections, Trinity College Dublin).**
Right: **Fig. 13. O'Neill lithograph of details of Moone High Cross (Special Collections, Trinity College Dublin).**

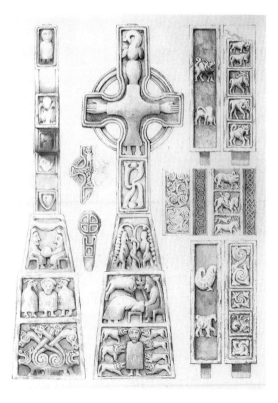

Far left: Pl. 27.
Moone: shaft, west
face.
Left: Pl. 28. Moone:
shaft, north side.
Below: Pl. 29.
Moone: base, east
face, showing Adam
and Eve.

Above: Pl. 30. Moone: base, east face, showing sacrifice of Isaac.
Below: Pl. 31. Moone: base, east face, showing Daniel in the lions' den.

And at the bottom a large panel is taken up with one of Christ's most memorable miracles: the feeding of the 5,000 with just five barley loaves and two small fishes (Pl. 39). The design is reduced to its essentials; the lack of a human figure suggests that the intended audience may already have been well aware of the story.

Pl. 32. Moone: base, west face, showing crucifix.

Pl. 33. Moone: base, west face, showing 12 apostles.

43

The inclusion of biblical scenes with fabulous beasts and the melding of pagan Celtic sagas with Christian Old and New Testament depictions seems to be incongruous, yet whimsical and delightful. The more austere leaders of reform movements may have disapproved of this blend: the biblical stories, after all, were to teach the illiterate the essential themes of the gospel. At any rate, as far as the present record shows, neither this particular blend of images nor the proportions of the cross itself would be reproduced elsewhere.

Pl. 34. Moone: base, north side, showing St Paul and St Anthony.

Pl. 35. Moone: base, north side, showing St Anthony tempted.

Pl. 36. Moone: base, north side, showing a fabulous beast.

Pl. 37. Moone: base, south side, showing three children in the fiery furnace.

Pl. 38. Moone: base, south side, showing flight into Egypt.

Pl. 39. Moone: base, south side, showing miracle of loaves and fishes.

CASTLEDERMOT, COUNTY KILDARE

The modern church and its ancient crosses lie within the town boundaries of Castledermot, about 12 kilometres south of Moone. A monastery was founded on this site in 812 by St Dermot, a member of the Céli Dé ascetic-renewal movement. It was plundered several times by Danish warriors, but continued to have influence until the tenth century, when further plundering occurred. According to Lewis,[4] it was destroyed in the fourteenth century by the Scots under Edward Bruce,

Pl. 40.
Castledermot:
South Cross
seen through
Romanesque
doorway.

who also destroyed the town; Cromwell's men seized it in the war of 1641 and it never recovered. The modern Protestant (Anglican Church of Ireland) church was repaired in 1821. It is surprising, in light of this troubled past, how much of the churchyard and crosses remain. The crosses follow the general idiom of those at Graignamanagh, although they show considerably more sophistication. The space between ring and arms has now been cut through, as was seen also on the Cross at Moone.

Pl. 41.
Castledermot:
South Cross
seen through
Romanesque
doorway.

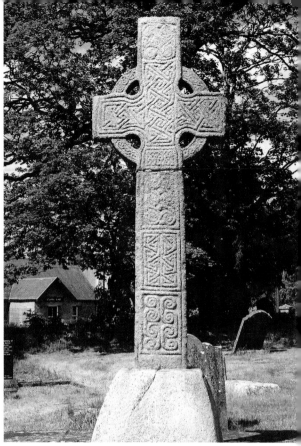

Above left: Pl. 42. Castledermot: South Cross, west face against the church.

Above right: Pl. 43. Castledermot: South Cross, east face.

Left: Pl. 44. Castledermot: South Cross, west face.

Above: Pl. 45. Castledermot: South Cross, head, west face.

South Cross

A glimpse of the South Cross can be seen though a restored Romanesque archway (Pl. 40) and against the more modern church (Pls 41 and 42). This cross is made up of three segments – the head, the shaft and the base – which were brought together in the nineteenth century.[5]

East Face

The east face (Pl. 43) is unusual in comparison with most of the crosses of this period in that it features no figured panels. The absence of figures leads to a comparison of

Pl. 46. Castledermot: South Cross, shaft, west face.

Pl. 47. Castledermot: South Cross, head, north side.

Pl. 48. Castledermot: South Cross, shaft, north side.

Right: Pl. 49. Castledermot: South Cross, south side.
Below: Pl. 50. Castledermot: South Cross, base, west face.

this cross with the North Cross at Graignamanagh, but this one is of altogether finer craftsmanship. The centre of the head is occupied by a vertical fret pattern, which becomes horizontal to occupy the arms. At the top are four spirals coming out of a central plain area. Below the central motif is a small panel containing interlacing.

The shaft consists of a series of three panels. The bottom is made up of eight spirals, the middle of angular fretwork and the top, which is much worn, possibly shows six spirals. The ring has a fine sequence of running spirals; the base is uncarved.

West Face

This shows the crucifixion in the centre, with the two soldiers on each side (Pls 44 and 45). Above, two angels keep Christ company. David playing his harp is depicted on the left arm; on the right, Isaac awaits sacrifice. Above the centre there is a panel of three figures, unidentified. Above them, at the top, Christ is portrayed being flogged during the time of his trial. Below the crucifixion is a small damaged panel that shows the remnants of three figures, unidentified.

50

Above: Pl. 51. Castledermot: South Cross, base, south side.
Left: Pl. 52. Castledermot: South Cross, base, north side.

There appears to be no chronological sequence in the pictures displayed on the shaft. On the lowest panel is shown Daniel in the lions' den (from the Old Testament). The panel immediately above shows St Anthony in the desert, being tempted. This is a post-biblical story of asceticism. Next on the shaft, Eve presents Adam with the apple under the tree of life. The snake coils toward Eve. In the top panel St Anthony and St Paul are seen breaking bread in the desert.

North Side
The end of the arm shows a human figure; at the top two spirals fill the panel (Pl. 47). The shaft is taken up with scenes from the life of David. At the bottom he occupies the panel alone. Above this, the two rather weathered panels show David encountering and then slaying Goliath. Above this he occupies the arm and, at the top of the shaft, Saul and David embrace (Pl. 48).

Pl. 53. Castledermot: North Cross,
south-east aspect.

Right: Pl. 54.
Castledermot: North
Cross, south-east aspect.
Far right: Pl. 55.
Castledermot: North
Cross, east face.

Left: Pl. 56. Castledermot: North Cross, west face.
Below: Pl. 57. Castledermot: North Cross, head, west face.

South Side

A human figure is shown on the end of the arm and three spirals occupy the top (Pl. 49). The shaft shows a series of panels portraying human figures. There are six panels, each containing two figures, representing the 12 apostles (five panels are shown in Pl. 50).

Base

As mentioned, the base is uncarved on the east face. The west face depicts a hunting scene, where the two human figures in profile are positioned one above the other, while the animals are arranged in three tiers. On each, a human figure with a spear or club chases a number of animals of varying shape: a goose, a pig and a stag, among others (Pl. 50).

On the south side, the base has a dramatic picture of the story of the feeding of the 5,000. Eight figures line the bottom of the panel – perhaps the beneficiaries of Christ's largesse. Christ is seen extending his arm toward the five barley loaves and the two small fishes. The panel is somewhat crooked, sloping down to the right (Pl. 51). The base on the north side shows an enigmatic picture of two people in close encounter, perhaps fighting or embracing one another (Pl. 52).

North Cross

Here it is the proportions that are unusual, as the two-tiered base is quite large in comparison to the head and shaft. The shaft sits slightly askew on its base, and a narrow recessed band may represent the joining of the two portions. Altogether, the cross appears chunky and seems to have been made by someone less skilled than the carvers of other high crosses, including the South Cross on this same site. The

Left: Pl. 58. Castledermot: North Cross, south side.
Below: Pl. 59. Castledermot: North Cross, shaft, south side.

general appearance can best be seen in oblique views, such as in Plates 53 and 54. The ring is decorated by wavy lines and spirals in a variety of configurations.

East Face

The focus here is on the crucifixion (Pls 53 and 55). Two soldiers stand on each side; angels fly above Christ's outstretched arms. A flat plate-like shape above Christ's head may represent the crown of thorns. The four panels surrounding the crucifixion show three figures each, representing the 12 apostles. At the bottom of the shaft (Pl. 55) one sees two figures, which have not been identified. In the central panel are St Paul and St Anthony breaking bread in the desert. Three further unidentified figures occupy the top panel of the shaft.

Pl. 60. Castledermot: North Cross, base, east face.

Pl. 61. Castledermot: North Cross, base, west face.

Pl. 62. Castledermot: North Cross,
base, north side.

West Face

The central focus on this face of the cross is on our first parents, as told in Genesis. Eve presents Adam with the apple, under the branch of the tree of knowledge. The serpent coils from the tree trunk to Eve (Pls 56 and 57). On the north arm David plays his harp and on the south Isaac is bent to receive the blow from Abraham; the ram lies above them. At the head of the cross there is a portrayal of the judgement of Solomon. A central upside-down figure represents the child spared by its true mother after Solomon has threatened to split it in two.

The shaft has only three panels (Pl. 56). The panel at the bottom of the shaft shows three unidentified figures; the one above it is hard to make out but may represent St Anthony in the desert. The top panel quite clearly shows Daniel, flanked by two lions.

South Side

The south side (Pl. 58) is decorated with such broad interlacing that five circles, connected with diagonal bands, occupy the whole surface in one panel. The end of the arm is decorated with an equally thick band in a meandering symmetrical pattern.

North Side

The north side (Pl. 59) is filled with a series of interconnected spirals.

Pl. 63. Castledermot: North Cross, base, south side.

Base

The base of the North Cross has a large sloping plinth, showing signs of damage on its upper surface. The plinth on the west and south sides is covered in a series of spirals and with C-scrolls on the east face. The east and west surfaces of the base proper are covered in coarse spirals – twelve on the west side and nine on the east (Pls 60 and 61). On the north side of the base (Pl. 62) is a strange, unidentified crouching figure, holding its legs (the plinth is indecipherable). On the south side there is a clear depiction of the figure of Christ at the miracle of feeding the 5,000 by dividing up five barley loaves and two small fishes (Pl. 63).

1. Herity, Michael, 'The Context and Date of the High Crosses at Dísert Diarmada (Castledermot), Co. Kildare' in Etienne Rynne (ed.), *Figures from the Past* (Dublin: Glendale Press, 1987), p. 111.

2. Harbison, Peter, *Guide to National and Historic Monuments of Ireland* (3rd ed., Dublin: Gill and Macmillan, 2001), p. 197.

3. Fitzgerald, Walter, 'Report of the Local Secretary, Co. Kildare: the Restoration of the High Cross at Moone' in *Journal of the Royal Society of Antiquaries of Ireland*, vol. xxiv (1894), pp 75–6.

4. Lewis, Samuel, *Atlas Comprising the Counties of Ireland and a General Map of the Kingdom* (vol. i, London: S. Lewis, 1837), p. 295.

5. Harbison, Peter, *The High Crosses of Ireland: An Iconographical and Photographic Survey* (vol. i, Bonn: Dr Rudolf Habelt GMBH, 1992), p. 39.

Chapter 4

The High Crosses of Ossory

Not far from the granite crosses examined in the last chapter, in a south-westerly direction, are a number of crosses that appear very different in style and decoration from those to be found elsewhere. These are located in three separate sites, on both sides of the Kilkenny–Tipperary border. As they are all in the diocese of Ossory, the name Ossory, taken from the ancient kingdom located in that region, seems appropriate for this group of crosses.

The crosses are to be found at three sites – Ahenny, Kilkieran and Killamery. They are all made of sandstone, which would have been easier for the mason to work than granite. They have recently been dated to a more recent point in time than the Barrow Valley crosses, and more closely approximated to the scriptural crosses of the later ninth and tenth centuries.[1] One of the problems with dating comes from the fact that some of the crosses may have been reassembled over the years. An earlier shaft, for example, might have been placed on a later base, making definitive dating difficult. Certainly, the odd conical caps to be seen on most of the crosses in this group were discovered some years ago, lying around in the graveyard, and were placed arbitrarily on the heads of the crosses, where they can be seen today. It is likely that earlier versions of these crosses, as elsewhere, were made of wood and carried in procession or used as boundary markers.

The crosses of this region are remarkably similar in shape and very different from those in other parts of the country. Most remarkable is the proportion of the ring to the cross: it is much larger than has hitherto been seen and dominates the structure. Also of interest is the absence of figurative art on the cross itself, although on some the base is carved with human and animal crowd scenes. Celtic designs occupy the head and the shaft on all faces. Interlacing of great variety and complexity occupies the faces of the crosses. Each is framed in raised moulding. Helen M. Roe[2] points out that the decoration of these unique high crosses includes all the most basic motifs of non-figurative Irish Christian art. The crosses are all graced with a capping of some sort. This sometimes looks like a little roof, as in the case of the cross at

Pl. 64. Ahenny: view from east.

Killamery, and at other places it resembles a tall cloche. In one instance, the South Cross at Ahenny, it has been reduced to a thin skim-stone cap.

The Ahenny site is said to be that of an ancient monastery, founded by St Crispin.[3] Nothing now remains of any church building. Looking across the green fields towards the site, in the first photograph (Pl. 64), two crosses may be seen in a graveyard amid green fields. The second picture (Pl. 65) is taken from inside the graveyard. In addition to the two crosses of interest, there are several horizontal slabs and a few modern headstones.

Ahenny, County Tipperary

The crosses are designated the North Cross and the South Cross. The North Cross can be easily recognised by the missing section of the ring.

North Cross

Beneath the prominent beehive-like cap, the cross shape takes on a structure common to other Ossory crosses, with scalloped indents where the horizontal arms meet the vertical shaft. The lower south arc of the ring is missing.

East Face

On the east face (Pls 66 and 68) the head of the cross is outlined by a rope-like border and filled with delicate and precise interlacing. This surrounds five convex bosses. The ring on the head is ornamented with a sequence of spirals. Below, on the shaft, are four spirals joined by diagonals and enclosing three birds' heads (Pl. 70). In the centre is a fifth spiral with four low-relief bosses within. Lower on the shaft is a contrasting panel of geometrical shape, with nine boxes side by side, each containing four smaller boxes (Pl. 71). Lowest on the shaft, on the slightly wider plinth, is a series of three spirals.

Above: Pl. 65. Ahenny: view from churchyard.
Left: Pl. 66. Ahenny: North Cross, east face.

Pl. 67. Ahenny: North Cross, west face.

Pl. 68.
Ahenny:
North Cross,
head, east
face.

Pl. 69. Ahenny:
North Cross, head,
west face.

Pl. 70. Ahenny: North
Cross, centre panel of east
face.

Pl. 71. Ahenny: North Cross,
lower panel of east face,
including spirals.

Right: Pl. 72. Ahenny: North Cross, shaft, west face, including interlacing on plinth.

Left: Pl. 73. Ahenny: North Cross, south side.

West Face

On the west face (Pls 67, 69 and 72) the decoration on the cross is less distinct and appears to be formed by paired spirals set among stippled bosses. The upper panel on the shaft shows interlacing of a coarser (yet symmetrical) type, with small head-like features at each corner. Below is a geometrical diamond pattern with an enclosed box of ribboned interlacing. The diamond pattern shows a balance between form and background, with each tiny centre empty. The lowest part of the shaft, again somewhat expanded, is decorated with a diagonal geometric pattern. The plinth is divided into a series of ten areas of interlacing.

North and South Sides
The south side of the cross shows the fine interjoining spiral on the shaft (Pl. 73).
The north side is similar.

Above: Pl. 74. Ahenny: North Cross, base, east face.
Below: Pl. 75. Ahenny: North Cross, base, west face.

Base

The square base is almost as wide as the arms. On the east side is a man under a tree, facing a variety of creatures. This may be Adam naming the animals (Pl. 74). On the west, the figure of the raised Christ faces us in the centre and appears with six apostles or bishops in profile, carrying pastoral staffs (Pl. 75). The south side of the base shows a funeral procession – a headless body placed upon a horse. Behind them, a man carries a human head, possibly that of the body being buried.

Pl. 76. Ahenny: North Cross, base, south side.

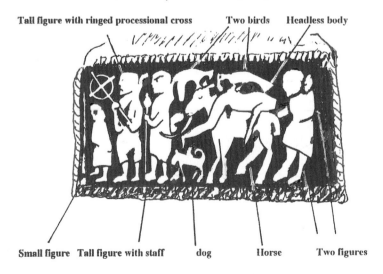

Fig. 14. Ahenny: North Cross, sketch of procession on base, south side.

In front are three men and a dog, with the leader carrying a processional cross. This remarkable scene has been variously interpreted: it may be a memorial to Goliath's death or, alternatively, to John the Baptist's (Pl. 76; a sketch, Fig. 14, is included to identify the figures).[3] The base's north side shows a procession of riders and a chariot. It has not been photographed, as it is now rather indistinct.

South Cross

The South Cross has an intact ring. The cap is a mere irregular sliver. The overall configuration of this cross is similar to that of the North Cross. However, the interlacing has subtle differences and the base is plain.

Pl. 77. Ahenny: South Cross, east face.

Pl. 78. Ahenny: South Cross, west face.

East Face

On the east face (Pl. 77), the interlacing at the top of the shaft resembles open wickerwork, balancing the space taken up by the ribboning with that of the background. On the head, the interlacing moves from loose to tight toward the central boss. All five bosses are flat, with ringed surfaces. Lower on the shaft is a pattern of five spirals, similar to that on the North Cross, each with a bird-like head in the centre.

West Face

At the top of the cross, four sections of interlacing, connected by diagonals, form semi-circular curves with their backs to each other (Pl. 78). The bosses are raised and round. Around the central boss the interlacing is somewhat more irregular than on the other side and loses some of its definition as it approaches each boss. Further down on the shaft are two sets of five spirals, with the central one showing small differences (Pl. 80). To be noted on the head ring are the differences between the upper and lower halves. The top half features interlacing, while the bottom features interconnected pairs of spirals.

Left: Pl. 79. Ahenny: South Cross, details of shaft, east face.

Right: Pl. 80. Ahenny: South Cross, details of shaft, west facc.

North and South Sides

The sides show a marvellous variety of interlacing, back-to-back spirals and geometrical diagonal lines. Those on the south side are shown (Pls 81 and 82).

Pl. 81. Ahenny: South
Cross, with North
Cross in distance.

Pl. 82. Ahenny: South
Cross, south side with
shaft detail.

KILKIERAN, COUNTY KILKENNY

This ancient church site holds three crosses. All of these can be seen in Plate 83.

East Cross

The East Cross is a slender shaft with a narrow cross piece (Pl. 84). The arms are short, their edges notched at the centre. Similar notches occur on the shaft above and below the central piece. The base is round and undecorated. Were it not for the company it keeps it would not qualify as a high cross at all.

South Cross

The South Cross is unornamented except for squared-off mouldings along the edges of the shaft and arms. The ring extends almost to the edges of the arms and has no moulding. A substantial cap sits on top of the head. The base is plain. It may have served as a prototype for the others in the region (Pls 85 and 86).

Above: Pl. 83. Kilkieran: church site with three crosses.
Left: Pl. 84. Kilkieran: East Cross.

Pl. 85. Kilkieran: South Cross, east face.

Pl. 86. Kilkieran: South Cross, west face.

West Cross

In contrast to the other crosses in this churchyard, many Celtic designs are shown on the West Cross – including the base, of which one side features carvings of horses. Thick roping edges the head on both sides, with those on the west face showing faint remnants of the original 'coil'. The edges are missing from the shaft on both faces. In order to compare the decorations on each face they are described together (Pls 87 and 88). Both aspects of the head and arms are filled with interlacings. On the east face this forms a continuous ribbon, while on the west face it is much finer. It divides into a number of sections above the centre before flowing into a fine network over the rest of the head.

The ring is carved with a single interlaced coil. The beehive-shaped capstone is ringed near its centre and bulges at its lower end. It is slightly larger than a comparable one at Ahenny (the North Cross: Pl. 67, p. 82).

Right: Pl. 87. Kilkieran: West Cross,
east face.
Below: Pl. 88. Kilkieran: West Cross,
west face.
Below right: Pl. 89. Kilkieran: West Cross,
shaft, west face.

East and West Faces

The east-face shaft has been damaged and the details of the panels are marred. The upper part has six medallions or spirals, and the lower has fine interlacing (Pl. 87). The shaft on the west face also has two panels (Pls 88 and 89). The carving is considerably more distinct than that on the east face. The upper part shows six tight, solid spirals; the lower part, while roughly symmetrical, has an unusual pattern of thick spirals around a small central cross.

Pl. 90. Kilkieran: West Cross, base, east face.

Pl. 91. Kilkieran: West Cross, base, west face.

Pl. 92. Kilkieran: West Cross,
north side.

Pl. 93. Kilkieran: West Cross,
south side.

Base

The east face of the base is carved with a procession of headless riders and their horses. Owing to the difficulty in photographing this through an adjacent iron railing, not all of the eight horses are shown (Pl. 90). The other three surfaces are covered in panels of interlacing. The west face (Pl. 91) has three panels, the centre showing five spirals, and on the north side the interlacing is arranged in three rows (Pl. 92).

North and South Sides

The north and south sides show tightly symmetrical interlacing within the spaces left by the broken-off edge ropings on the shaft and less prominent borders on the base (Pls 92 and 93).

Thus the only cross at Kilkieran to show ornamentation has just one panel of figurative art, and it is doubtful that this represents a Bible scene. It is most remarkable for its resemblance to the Ahenny crosses, only a few miles away, in similar territory.

Pl. 94. Killamery Cross and ruined church.

KILLAMERY, COUNTY KILKENNY

Set in an old churchyard a few miles north of the other two Ossory sites is the single sandstone high cross of Killamery (Pl. 94). In overall proportion, the head and arms are on a smaller scale than those at Ahenny, and the cross stands a little taller. The cap takes the form of a little roof, unique among the Ossory crosses but common in the later crosses of the midlands.

East Face

On the east face (Pl. 95), the head features a spread-eagled beast within the border, and beneath this a solid rounded boss takes up the centre spot. Extending on each side into the two arms are a large snake and a small snake, eating at one another (Pl. 97). The tails of the larger snake coil upwards into a single spiral, while the tails of the smaller snakes descend to form intricate interlacing on the upper part of the shaft. Beneath this are three flowers, each with four diagonally placed petals.

Pl. 95. Killamery: east face.

Pl. 96. Killamery: west face.

West Face

The west face (Pl. 96) is much eroded, but a whorl on the centre, in place of a boss, can clearly be seen. Below it an indistinct carving of figures is believed to show God blessing and sanctifying the seventh day, as told in Genesis.[4] Others believe the carving to show a scene of crucifixion. Whether it tells of the beginning of the world or of human redemption, it must have conveyed a powerful message. The ends of the arms of the cross show hunting scenes. The shaft has two contrasting panels of fretwork.

Base

The base is unusual in that it is composed of three tiers, the uppermost being broader above than below. The middle tier on the west side shows a series of six bosses separated by ill-defined interlacing.

Pl. 97. Killamery: head, east face.

Of all the Ossory crosses now in existence, the one at Killamery shows the finest details and balance. It provides a fitting conclusion to the examination of crosses that display a preponderance of Celtic patterns, showing to what heights of excellence this particular design could reach. Now we turn the pages to the series of scriptural crosses that return to the stories of the Bible in the tradition of those we have seen at Castledermot and Moone.

1. Harbison, Peter, *The High Crosses of Ireland: An Iconographical and Photographic Survey* (vol. i, Bonn: Dr Rudolf Habelt GMBH, 1992), p. 370.
2. Roe, Helen, *The High Crosses of Western Ossory* (Kilkenny: Kilkenny Archaeological and Historical Society, 1969).
3. Harbison *op. cit.*, p. 12.
4. *Ibid.*, p. 122.

Pl. 98. Termonfeckin: entrance to churchyard.

CHAPTER 5

———

SITES WITH A SINGLE SCRIPTURAL CROSS OF THE NINTH OR TENTH CENTURY

Scriptural high crosses in Ireland are noted for blending figurative art portraying the highlights of Old and New Testament with abstract patterns derived from Celtic sources. These patterns form the ground upon which the scriptural figures are revealed.

The first site to be visited in this chapter, at Termonfeckin in County Louth, singles out only the two essential messages of the Christian gospel, namely the crucifixion and the risen Christ. The rest of the cross is covered with Celtic patterning. Other crosses go into great detail in portraying those scenes held to be most relevant from both testaments. Those scriptural crosses now standing on their own – at Termonfeckin, Drumcliff, Ardboe, Donaghmore and Durrow – are included in this chapter.

The ninth and tenth centuries are particularly noted for the great flowering of Irish art in the form of high crosses. This is especially remarkable in view of the Viking raids that had started at the end of the eighth century and continued throughout the first half of the ninth century. Varying from short local raids along the sea coast to more serious incursions inland, the Vikings met stiff opposition and eventually withdrew back across the Irish Sea, at least for a time. According to Scherman[1] and to Harbison,[2] the inspiration for the high crosses arose in the wake of a religious revival movement called Céli Dé, or Culdee – servants of God. Leaders such as St Maelruin of Tallaght brought about a campaign of reform to counteract the laxity of the church, which had become a problem during the seventh century. They preached a return to the asceticism of the early monastic ideal. This movement denounced wealth and worldliness and emphasised piety, asceticism and discipline within the church membership and pastoral care and education for the lay countrymen.

Numerous illuminated manuscripts were created. These were primarily available to the monks and nuns within the walls of the monasteries and to those who could read. However, they were often lost through looting or burning by the invading

Vikings. Looking for a way to preserve the sacred stories and to educate the illiterate laity, the monks began to have these stories carved on the stone crosses, already a tradition, and post them at the boundaries of the monasteries, where they were easily accessible. As the genre evolved, they changed from being almost wholly decorative: they came to include in graphic detail the essential themes of the Christian faith and its source, the Old Testament. The particular format we have seen on the Castledermot crosses was further developed into a form of high art. The crosses' masons did not abandon their Celtic decorations after the reform, but instead blended panels of the scriptural figurative carvings amongst panels of filigree and interlacing, creating a harmonious whole – and, indeed, creating something unique in the field of Christian art. The proportion of figurative art to Celtic interlacing patterns ranges from crosses with single biblical representations amidst a profusion of Celtic art to crosses where the Old and New Testament stories predominate over the interlacing.

In our own day, while the Celtic interlacing can be appreciated even when severely worn down by weathering, many of the figured panels have lost much of their definition and are now difficult to identify. Others, because of the quality of the stone and the clarity of the carving, appear as if they had just recently left the mason's chisel. The crosses that are described in this section of the book have all

**Pl. 99. Termonfeckin High Cross:
east face.**

been attributed to the ninth and tenth centuries, with no clear evidence as to which date from earlier and which from later in this period. Those high crosses that appear singly on their sites will be described first. The sites containing whole groups of crosses will be described in later chapters.

We will start in the county of Louth, just north of the County Dublin sites of Tallaght and Finglas, where the Céli Dé movement started.

TERMONFECKIN, COUNTY LOUTH

St Fechin founded a monastery in this spot in the seventh century.[3] The parish church that occupies the site is relatively modern and under the auspices of the Church of Ireland (Anglican). The gate is open, showing the modern church up the driveway (Pl. 99). The cross lies off to the left, in the churchyard. According to Harbison, the sandstone high cross (over two metres high) dates back to the ninth century. It is finely proportioned, the height being two and a half times the width of the arms. The shaft slightly tapers to the top, which ends in a peaked shingled roof.

Pl. 100. Termonfeckin: west face.

Pl. 101. Termonfeckin: head,
east face.

Pl. 102. Termonfeckin: detail
of shaft, east face.

Above: Pl. 103. Termonfeckin:
head, east face.
Right: Pl. 104. Termonfeckin:
detail of shaft, west face.

East Face

On the east face (Pl. 99) of the cross head there is a carving, now rather ill defined, of Christ on the cross with a Roman soldier on each side. The gospel tells how one soldier plunged a sword into Christ's side and brought out both blood and water. The other offered Christ a sponge of wine vinegar to relieve his thirst. These two

Pl. 105. Termonfeckin: south and east aspects.

figures have been given names – not from the Bible, but from a Syriac manuscript of the sixth century.[4] The sword carrier is called Longinus, from the Greek word for lance, while the bearer of vinegar is called Stephaton. We will use these names here, for they appear many times on the crucifix carvings of the scriptural high crosses.

An angel can be seen above the crucifix. Single figures appear at each end of the arms. These cannot be identified with certainty. On the upper shaft one can dimly make out two human heads surrounded by irregular fine-curved mouldings, which end in spirals. The lower shaft is covered by fluidly carved irregular C-scrolls of singular beauty.

West Face

On the west face (Pl. 100), in the centre of the cross is a carving of the last judgement, with Christ in glory. Christ holds a sceptre in his right hand and a cross shaft in his left. Photography allows us to view these two sides together, so that we can see the sacrifice of Christ on one side and his transcendent glory on the other. These are the two most important statements of Christ's mission to redeem humankind, and common themes for the east and west faces of many of the more detailed scriptural crosses which will be shown later in this book.

The interlacing on the lower panel of the shaft is remarkable in contrast to the east face as it includes two panels carved with patterns of considerable precision. The upper panel, severely eroded, consists of 32 small squares split by diagonals. A crack runs through the panel, suggesting that the two pieces were once separated and have been reassembled. Below this, and showing little sign of weathering, the panel is filled with eight larger, circular areas of interlacing connected by diagonals. The current appearance of the east and west faces of the heads can be seen in Plates 101 and 103 respectively, and the decorations on the shafts are shown in Plates 102 and 104.

North and South Sides

A view of the cross from the south-eastern aspect gives a sense of the nobility of the overall monument. Its proportions and the fluidity of its design can be seen in Plate 105, which shows the south side and the interlacing on the ring margin. Further details of the south-side central cross within a circle and lower panel of interlacing are seen in Plate 106. The lower panel on the south side contains three circular bands of interlacing similar to the patterns on the west face. The interlacing of the lower panel on the north side shows variations on these themes; it is arranged in diagonals and spirals.

Above and right: Pl. 106.
Termonfeckin: details of
south side.

DRUMCLIFF, COUNTY SLIGO

Under bare Benbulben's head […]
By the road, an ancient cross.

These words by the poet W.B. Yeats[5] bring us north-west across Ireland to one of the most beautiful of all the high crosses. Harbison's guide[6] tells us that St Columba founded a monastery there in the sixth century. The sandstone cross was erected around the year 1000 CE. It stands attached at its base to a wall bordering the lane that leads up to the modern Protestant church.

Pl. 107. Drumcliff High Cross: east face with tower.

89

Pl. 108. Drumcliff:
west face with
church.

Pl. 109. Drumcliff:
head, east face.

Pl. 110.
Drumcliff: head,
west face.

The cross has several features that add to its beauty and delicacy and, indeed, to the sense of whimsy and delight it conveys. The proportions of the head, with its deeply scalloped arms, almost continuing the line of the ring, are particularly fine. The volutes, those strange rolls attached to the inner arcs of the arms, are so large that they seem to form the points of a square and to enfold the central figure. Adding to the delicacy of the carving is the border of beaded lines, which continues around the whole outline of the cross inside the solid moulding. The ring is embroidered with a variety of coils and spirals.

East Face
On the east face (Pls 107 and 109) the head has as its central image the figure of Christ in glory along with the apostles. The shaft portrays scenes from the Old Testament. Reading from the bottom up, which puts them in the order in which they are narrated in the Bible, are Adam and Eve (Pl. 111) (how sinuous the snake is!), then David slaying Goliath and, near the head, Daniel in the lions' den. Celtic interlacing in the form of tight circles occupies the panels below and above Adam and Eve. A lion in higher relief prances between a panel of interlacing and David slaying Goliath (Pl. 113).

Pl. 111. Drumcliff: shaft, east face, showing Adam and Eve.

Pl. 112. Drumcliff: shaft, west face, showing the naming of John.

West Face

On the west face (Pls 108 and 110) the crucifix occupies the centre of the head. Two heads appear on the arms, possibly those of the two thieves crucified with Christ. On the shaft, below the raised profile camel, is the New Testament story of the naming of John the Baptist, above a six-circled panel of interlacing (Pl. 112). At the top of the shaft we see a depiction of Christ in the hands of the authorities, being mocked. Above this panel is a plain band – a clear break in the continuity of the shaft, suggesting that two stones were used in the construction of this cross. The panel at the top of the shaft shows two figures, the identity of whom is not clear.

Of special note, and contributing to a sense of delight, are the raised carvings of strange animals that occupy the centre of each shaft. They seem to be ready to burst from the confines of the stone. The animal on the east face represents a lion (Pl. 113), and that on the west face represents a camel (Pl. 114). The lion appears ready to pounce. The camel appears somewhat hunched and at first sight rather bizarre. Our idea of a camel is that of the single-humped dromedary, with its gently curved underbelly. But the ancient nomads of the north-east Asian steppes were more familiar with the Bactrian camel, and it is this image the Drumcliff masons depicted. De Paor in his book *Ireland and Early Europe* indicates that Celtic art was influenced by the art forms of the Eurasian steppes, and this Sligo representation suggests that influence may have come from even further east.[7] Plate 115 shows, for comparison, the picture of a buckle plaque from southern Siberia of the second century BCE.[8]

Pl. 113. Drumcliff: shaft, east face, showing a lion.

Pl. 114. Drumcliff: shaft, west face, showing a camel.

Pl. 115. Buckle plaque from southern Siberia, showing Bactrian camels (from Arthur M. Sackler Foundation. Photo copyright Simon Feldman.)

Pl. 116. Drumcliff: south side, with Ben Bulben.

North and South Sides

A panoramic view of the south side takes in the remarkable shape of Ben Bulben (Pl. 116). Both sides of the cross have a variety of somewhat similar interlacing. On the shaft (Pls 117 and 118), the lowest pattern has a sequence of large and small spirals, alternating, and above this broad and narrow ribbons interlace. Two strange animals in contrasting poses face each other under the arms. We are back to whimsy.

Left: Pl. 117. Drumcliff: south side, upper panel.
Above: Pl. 118. Drumcliff: south side, lower panel.

ARDBOE AND DONAGHMORE, COUNTY TYRONE

Ardboe High Cross

The next cross of note, standing on its own, takes us into Northern Ireland, to the county of Tyrone on the western shore of Lough Neagh. According to the writer of *Historic Monuments of Northern Ireland*,[9] the Ardboe cross marks the site of

Pl. 119. Ardboe
High Cross in
silhouette.

Pl. 120. Ardboe: east face.

a monastery associated with St Colman, founded perhaps in the sixth century. The cross was re-erected in the mid-nineteenth century after it had fallen; it is made up of four blocks of red sandstone. At 5.7 metres high, it is one of the tallest high crosses now standing, being exceeded only by the Tall Cross at Monasterboice. It is also particularly slender (just over one metre across the arms). The cross is enclosed by a metal fence. Seen in silhouette in the early dawn (Pl. 119), it is indeed a dramatic monument. It stands outside a churchyard with modern grave plots and some ruined church buildings.

Severe weathering has affected all sides, making deciphering the scenes a matter of some guesswork. Despite the weathering – or perhaps because of it – there is a certain majestic mystical charm about this cross. The east face is affected more than the west. Part of the top and the north arc of the cross are gone and there are deep vertical creases in the frontal aspect of the upper segment of the head and the northern arm. The Ardboe high cross is noted for its wide variety of biblical stories. In the centre of the east face (Pls 120 and 122) is the last judgement with Christ in glory – a similar scene to that on the west face of the cross at Termonfeckin. At Ardboe it is the west face that shows the crucifixion (Pls 121 and 123).

97

Pl. 121. Ardboe: west face.

East Face

The panels on this face of the shaft portray salient stories from the Old Testament (Pl. 124). Reading from the bottom up, the lowest panel shows Adam and Eve conscious of their nakedness, then the sacrifice of Isaac, then Daniel in the lions' den. The panel above this is now so weathered as to be indecipherable. Next comes a box-like panel, slightly wider than the rest of the shaft. Above this the scales of judgement licked by flames are positioned above a number of human heads and the Christ figure, seen in Plate 122.

West Face

As mentioned above, the west side of the cross head shows the crucifixion with the two soldiers Longinus and Stephaton. The arms at each side are identical, with three figures each, and present the arrest of Jesus. The same figures appear just beneath the crucifix (Pl. 123). On the shaft (Pl. 125), again in ascending order, the tops of three figures representing the adoration of the three wise men and then the wedding feast at Cana may be made out. Above this (Pl. 126) there is a panel showing the multiplication of the loaves and fishes and then the entry of Christ into Jerusalem on a donkey.

Pl. 122. Ardboe: head,
east face.

North and South Sides

The shaft of the north side is now so weathered that no satisfactory pictures could
be taken. In earlier times this could be seen to portray scenes of Christ's childhood,
including his baptism, Christ among the doctors, the slaughter of the innocents
and the annunciation to the shepherds.[10] The head shows panels of interlacing
(Pl. 127).

On the south side the wider panel and the top of the shaft (Pl. 128) display
Celtic ornamentation, with four bosses on the wider panel surrounded by a layer
of beading on the less-weathered section above a diagonal crack. Four bosses, with

Right: Pl. 123. Ardboe: head, west face.
Below: Pl. 124. Ardboe: shaft, east face.
Below right: Pl. 125. Ardboe: west face, lower shaft.

100

Left: Pl. 126. Ardboe: west face, mid-shaft detail.

Right: Pl. 127. Ardboe: head, north side.

interlacing above and below, occupy the top panel. Bands of small interlacing circles occupy the underside of the ring arm. On the lower part of the shaft (Pl. 129), the scenes return to the Old Testament. Cain is seen in the act of slaying Abel at the foot of the shaft. The sculptors then skipped right to a post-Bible story, showing St Paul and Anthony breaking bread in the wilderness, with the raven feeding them from above. This represents a recognition of an asceticism implicit in the Desert Fathers' monastic tradition and promoted by the Céli Dé movement.

The high cross at Ardboe remains in 2007 much as it was in 1989, when the pictures of the west face were taken. There is no evidence at the site of attempts to restore or protect this ancient monument. Interestingly, a similar cross is to be found nearby, in the centre of the town of Donaghmore.

Pl. 128. Ardboe: head south side.   Pl. 129. Ardboe: south side.

Pl. 130. Donaghmore High
Cross, east face.

Pl. 131. Donaghmore:
replica of east face.

Donaghmore High Cross

Here the high cross is similarly weathered. However, the members of the local
historical society, according to a sign on the site, decided to erect an interpretative
replica in 2001. Two sets of photographs of the cross (Pls 130 and 132) are compared
here with two others of the replica (Pls 131 and 133). In general, the carvings on
the replica appear less full than on the original; however, the diamond shape on the
south side appears faithfully copied (Pls 132 and 133). Plate 134 shows the west face

103

above its adjacent wall. The scenes of Old and New Testament duplicate those of the Ardboe cross (for example, Adam and Eve, as shown in Plate 135). The rate of weathering can be seen by comparing a photograph of the sacrifice of Isaac (Pl. 136) taken in 1989 with one taken in 2006, along with the photographs of the replica.

Pl. 132. Donaghmore: south side.

Pl. 133. Donaghmore: replica of south side.

Left: Pl. 134. Donaghmore: west face.
Above: Pl. 135. Donaghmore: detail of west face, showing Adam and Eve.
Below: Pl. 136. Donaghmore: comparisons of detail of west face, showing sacrifice of Isaac. A: 1989; B: 2006; C: replica, 2006.

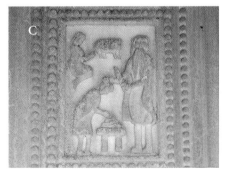

Durrow, County Laois

[handwritten: Offaly]

If ever there were a point to indicate the central spot of Ireland, it would be Durrow. It lies close to an ancient route, the post-glacial esker ridge that extends westward to the Shannon, where Clonmacnoise stands, and towards the east to the environs of Dublin and the coast. In former times, pilgrims and other travellers could walk or ride this trail above the bogs and forests covering the land to the north and south.

St Columba founded the monastery at Durrow in the sixth century.[11] A hundred years later, the illuminated *Book of Durrow* was produced here. That book is now in the library of Trinity College Dublin. Two hundred years after that the high cross was carved. This beautiful sandstone cross stood, when the photograph shown (Pl. 137) was taken (in 1989), in a gateway under some beech trees, amid grave slabs dating back to the time the monastery was flourishing – from its foundation until, perhaps, the eleventh century. According to the Office of Public Works,[12] who manage the site, the graveyard was the burial place for bishops, abbots and noblemen of the midlands and Munster. The grave slabs and cross made for a beautiful scene in that site but, for reasons of politics as well as of safety, it is to be moved to the nearby ruined church. Erosions and cracks mar the clarity of some of the carvings. The brownish tinge of the weathered stone is unusual and adds to this cross's uniqueness.

Pl. 138. Durrow: east face, under beech tree.

Pl. 139. Durrow: east face, close up.

East Face

At the centre of the head (Pls 139 and 140) is seen Christ in glory, with cross staff and sceptre. He stands on tightly woven interlacing, perhaps representing clouds. Above Christ's head is the lamb of God in a circle and above that are three bosses with interlinking ribbons. A gabled roof tops the cross. On each side are angels; the one on the south arm plays a pipe. David is featured at each end of the arms – playing the harp on the left and killing a lion on the right.

On the shaft (Pl. 141), reading from the bottom up, we see the raised Christ with two accompanying angels above two apostles. Above this is a Celtic design of four circles filled with interlacing and at the top is a carving of the sacrifice of Isaac.

Pl. 140. Durrow: head, east face.

Pl. 141. Durrow: shaft, east face.   Pl. 142. Durrow: west face.

West Face

The centre here is occupied by the figure of Christ with arms extended as if on the cross (Pls 142 and 143). We do not see any outline of a cross (other than the monument as a whole), but the meaning of the figure is clear. The two soldiers Longinus and Stephaton are present, jammed into a tight space within the cross's scalloped angles. Above, as noted by Harbison in 1970,[13] three figures represent Christ handing the keys of the kingdom to Peter, accompanied by Paul. The indistinct figures to right and left at the end of the arms represent Peter's denial of Jesus and Pilate washing his hands, according to the same authority. On the shaft, again reading from the bottom (Pl. 144), Christ is shown in the tomb, guarded by two soldiers. Above this are two panels dealing with Christ at the hands of the Roman authorities: first he is mocked; then, after his death, the soldiers cast lots for his garments. The ring has four bosses alternating with interlacing in each of the arcs.

Above: Pl. 143. Durrow: head, west face.
Right: Pl. 144. Durrow: shaft, west face.

Left and far left: Pl. 145.
Durrow: north side.

North Side

The lower panel (Pl. 145) shows two figures in embrace: perhaps John the Baptist and Christ. In the centre is a panel filled with two sets of four spirals. The lines deceive the viewer: looking laterally, each set appears back to back; looking from above to below, the spirals face each other and the bosses in each set are back to back. In the top panel of the shaft is a carving of a couple holding a child: Zacharias and Elizabeth with the infant John.

Under the ring (Pl. 146) is an unexpected and mystifying picture within the C-scroll border. A long snake with its head to the left and tail to the right coils around three heads. A similar image is seen under the south arm. The snake is not the lean and shrunken serpent that tempted Adam and Eve but a succulent, healthy reptile. The anatomical accuracy is surprising since Ireland has had no snakes since the Ice Age.[14] One must hunt through the literature for a satisfactory explanation of the meaning of this emblem. Miranda Green, in her book *Animals in Celtic Life and Myth*,[15] notes:

> Snakes possess complex symbolism in the Romano-Celtic world, evoking images of water, fertility, death and regeneration [. ...] The association of snakes with healing and renewal came about because of their sloughing their skins several times a year, apparently being reborn [. …] The snake is frequently a companion of the Goddess who herself has a clear identity as a spirit of fecundity, abundance or healing.

Pl. 146. Durrow: north side, under ring arc.

Pl. 147. Durrow: north side,
end of arm and top.

In Greek mythology, the familiar caduceus of Asclepius, although of different form, with the snakes' heads facing each other at the same end, is also a sign of healing.

As for the entwined human heads, one can speculate that the snakes are seen as embracing humankind, bringing health and revitalisation. If this meaning is valid then the scriptural crosses truly reflect the blending of Celtic and, indeed, eastern Mediterranean mythology with the stories of the Old and New Testament. With variations, the snake and human-head emblems recur on the other two main scriptural crosses, at Clonmacnoise and Monasterboice, giving the motifs added significance.

Pl. 148. Durrow: shaft, south side.

On the top of the cross's head on the north side is an unidentified figure. In the triangle of the gable roof is a boss with spirals and interlacing. Note that the gable roof has finials on it such as were to be found on wooden church gables of the same period.[16]

South Side

The south side (Pl. 148) has at the lower end of its shaft a depiction of Adam and Eve, then Cain slaying Abel. Above this panel is a warrior with two dogs (Pl. 149). Under the ring the snake emblem with three human heads can again be seen.

113

Durrow has given an example of a scriptural cross in a single setting. The next three chapters will deal with groups of crosses in each site. Durrow is placed in the mid-section of that great post-glacial ridge, the east–west esker. The route of this survey now progresses westward along that ridge to the shores of the mighty Shannon River and the ancient monastic site of Clonmacnoise.

Pl. 149. Durrow: south side, under ring arc.

1. Scherman, Katharine, *The Flowering of Ireland* (London: Little, Brown, 1981), p. 207.

2. Harbison, Peter, *The Golden Age of Irish Art: The Medieval Acheivement 600–1200* (London: Thames and Hudson, 1999), p. 152.

3. Harbison, Peter, *Pilgrimage in Ireland: The Monuments and the People* (New York: Syracuse University Press, 1991), p. 185.

4. Metford J.C.J., *Dictionary of Christian Lore and Legend* (London: Thames and Hudson, 1983), p. 162.

5. Rosenthal, M.L. (ed.), *Selected Poems of William Butler Yeats* (Basingstoke: Macmillan, 1962), p. 193.

6. Harbison, Peter, *Guide to National and Historic Monuments of Ireland* (3rd ed., Dublin: Gill and Macmillan, 2001), p. 291.

7. de Paor, Liam, *Ireland and Early Europe* (Dublin: Four Courts Press, 1997), p. 36.

8. Buckle, 2nd century BCE, from the Arthur M. Sackler Foundation, New York. Photo by Simon Feldman.

9. Department of the Environment for Northern Ireland, *Historic Monuments of Northern Ireland* (Belfast, 1983), p. 140.

10. Harbison 1999 *op. cit.*, p. 117.

11. Harbison 2001 *op. cit.*, p. 279.

12. Office of Public Works: www.opw.ie (2005).

13. Harbison, *Guide to the National Monuments of the Republic of Ireland* (Dublin: Gill and Macmillan, 1970), p. 204.

14. Scherman *op. cit.*, p. 94.

15. Green, Miranda, *Animals in Celtic Life and Myth* (London: Routledge, 1992) pp 164 and 224.

16. Hughes, Kathleen and Hamlin, Ann, *Celtic Monasticism: The Modern Traveller to the Early Irish Church* (New York: Seabury Press, 1981) p. 59.

CHAPTER 6

CLONMACNOISE:
WHERE THE STATELY SHANNON FLOWS

In olden times there may have been many sites in Ireland displaying multiple high crosses. In some of the areas already covered in this book, fragments of crosses (not presented here) remain to attest to the likelihood of many others having been lost or destroyed through the ages. It is fortunate that, in three locations at least, the magnificence of the ninth- and tenth-century crosses remains, with several at each site. Here, to start with, are those at Clonmacnoise.

> In a quiet watered land, a land of roses,
> Stands St Ciaran's city fair.
> And the warriors of Erin, in their famous generations,
> Slumber there.

T.W. Rolleston's translation[1] from the fourteenth-century Irish of Angus O'Gillan paints in a few words the sense of tranquillity that pervades this beautiful place on the banks of the mighty Shannon, the longest river in all the British Islands. The peace to be felt here is at odds with the site's turbulent history. According to Harbison,[2] the monastery was plundered and burned dozens of times both before and after the Norman invasion. In 1552 the English garrison took all the monastic valuables away, and the monastery never recovered. Even in our own time, the site has become too popular for its own good. Some of the flat grave slabs were being chipped for souvenirs so, along with the original crosses, they have been removed into the Interpretative Centre for protection. The latter are now represented outdoors by copies.

The site was no doubt chosen for its easy accessibility. The Shannon provided a waterway going south and north. The esker ridge left by the Ice Age extending from the east coast through Durrow to the Shannon provided a dry pathway above the bogs and through the forests. It also formed a shallow fording place under the Shannon water, which enabled travellers to forge further west into what is now

Connemara. It is at Clonmacnoise that the area's limestone underlay comes to the surface to provide the bedrock. But the crosses are not made of limestone. Instead the carvers chose other materials: millstone grit for the Cross of the Scriptures and sandstone for the plainer and earlier North Cross.

The monastery was set up in the sixth century by St Ciaran, who survived only six months, dying of a yellow plague, which devastated the country at that time. As Katherine Scherman states,[3] the school St Ciaran founded was to become, by the ninth century, one of the most illustrious seats of learning in the Christian world. It is the earliest recorded place of pilgrimage in Ireland, as the accounts of the *Annals of the Four Masters* and the *Annals of Clonmacnoise* report.[4] The layout as it may have been in its heyday is illustrated in Figure 4 (p. 27). It included many relatively small churches and chapels and, with the houses for the monks, workers, and other inhabitants, as well as hostels for pilgrims, would have had over a hundred buildings within its walls. Further buildings were reserved for women of the church around the Nuns' Chapel, a few hundred metres to the west.

The main group of photographs in this chapter (starting with Pl. 150) were taken outside in the churchyard in 1989. Some were taken of copies or replicas, in 2006 (and will be so indicated).

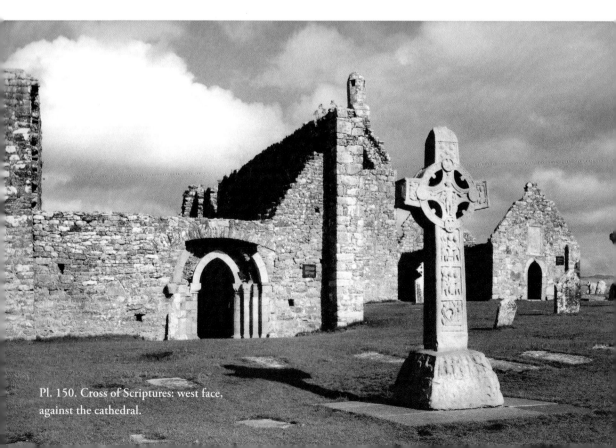

Pl. 150. *Cross of Scriptures: west face, against the cathedral.*

Cross of the Scriptures

As mentioned earlier, the high crosses have been removed to the safety of the Interpretative Centre. In their place, outside, faithful copies have been erected. The care that has been taken to replicate the carving in all its detail of style and scale can be seen by comparing a photo taken in 1989 of the head of the Cross of the Scriptures (Pl. 151) with that of the replica taken in 2006 against a background of the awning covering the cathedral during its restoration (Pl. 152).

The most outstanding monument is the beautiful early-tenth-century Cross of the Scriptures, seen in 1989 standing outside the cathedral, which was erected at about the same time. Additions or modifications such as the west door, decorated in the Romanesque style, are of twelfth-century date.[5] A sequence of photographs shows the Cross of the Scriptures in relation to the round tower and its proximity

Pl. 151. Cross of Scriptures, original, west face.

Pl. 152. Cross of Scriptures: replica, west face.

119

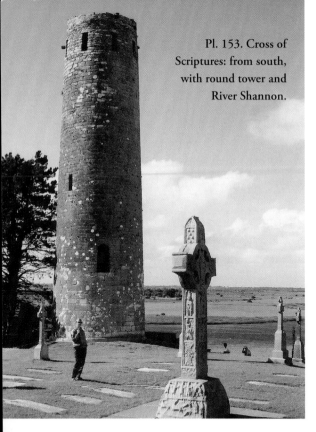

Pl. 153. Cross of Scriptures: from south, with round tower and River Shannon.

Pl. 154. Cross of Scriptures: from south-west, with smaller round tower.

Pl. 155. Cross of Scriptures: east face framed in arch, in fine weather.

Pl. 156. Cross of Scriptures: east face framed in arch, in wet weather.

Pl. 157. Cross of Scriptures: east face.   Pl. 158. Cross of Scriptures: west face.

to the River Shannon (Pl. 153) as well as to a smaller round tower (Pl. 154). When standing inside the cathedral, its door provides a frame for the cross, looking west, in fine weather (Pl. 155) and in rain (Pl. 156).

The Cross of the Scriptures is distinguishable from all other extant crosses by its slightly upturned arms. The ring meets the attenuations of the cross arms at their point of narrowing, so that the proportions of the arms and ring form a uniquely balanced whole. Small roundels containing spirals grace each junction of the ring with the arms and shaft on the east face, while similarly placed bosses on the west face are plain. The volutes are sited on the inside of the ring, as is the case with the crosses at Ardboe, Donaghmore and Durrow.

East Face

On the east face (Pls 157 and 159) a depiction of the last judgement can be made out, and above this, outside the ring, are three figures. The figure in the centre of these appears to be Christ, with either angels or apostles on each side. The top of the cross has a gabled roof. The arms contain small human figures. On the shaft (Pl. 161), the interpretation of the two lower panels is a matter of some doubt.

Right: Pl. 159. Cross of
Scriptures:head, east face.
Below: Pl. 160. Cross of
Scriptures: head, west face.

They may represent Joseph's life in Egypt as related in the book of Genesis (39–40), or perhaps portraits of notable figures from contemporary Irish history. Peter Harbison refers to these two contrasting interpretations.[6] The upper panel is most likely to portray Christ handing the keys of the kingdom to St Peter and a book to St Paul.

West Face

On the west face (Pls 158 and 160) the crucifix is in the centre of the head with the two soldiers connected with Christ's death, as seen on several crosses we have already examined. On each arm, kneeling figures face Christ. The identification of the panels on the shaft (Pl. 162) has proved easier than the identification of those on the east face. However, the scenes of the Christ's Passion are out of chronological order. Firstly, the middle panel depicts the seizing of Christ; then, at the top, the soldiers cast lots over his garments. At the bottom, Christ is seen in the tomb, over which are depicted the sleepy guards.

Left and far left: Pl. 161. Cross of Scriptures: details of shaft, east face.

Pl. 162. Cross of Scriptures: detail of shaft, west face.

Pl. 163. Cross of Scriptures: north side, upper panel.

Pl. 164. Cross of Scriptures: north side, lower panel.

North Side

On the north side (Pls 163 and 164) the themes portray the lives of the desert hermits, with St Anthony in the lower panel; the centre shows a figure playing a pipe, accompanied by two lions. The legend tells of how these lions helped to dig the grave of St Paul, so the suggestion is that St Anthony is playing a lamentation.[7] Above, a saint stands above the seated St Paul. The single snake occupies the space under the ring encircling only two heads, between borders of interlacing. Above is a cat with its prey. The end of the arm is raised in a flattened pyramid shape and the top shows a number of bosses. This part of the cross is similar to the south side (see Pl. 165).

124

South Side

The south side of the shaft is shown in its entirety in Plate 165. The single example on this particular cross of a full panel of interlacing is seen on the lowest panel (Pl. 166). To be noted at the ends of the diagonals are the small human heads with the remnants of tiny spirals on each side. Above this panel are scriptural themes (Pl. 167). In the middle David plays a lyre and, above this, the top panel represents David as a shepherd, watched over by an angel. Under the ring (Pl. 168) the snake motif appears once more, this time with two shorter snakes, around two heads. Above is the open hand of God.

The end of the south side (see the whole cross, Pl. 165) is in the form of a low pyramid. Above, at the top, are six bosses and, in the angle of the gable, some worn remnants of interlacing.

Left: Pl. 165. Cross of Scriptures: south side.
Above: Pl. 166. Cross of Scriptures: south side, lower panel.

125

Base

The base of the Cross of the Scriptures is more worn than the main part. Its slight slope might mean that it retains rain water for somewhat longer or that it is made of softer stone. The base on the east face (Pl. 169) shows a two-level procession, heading in different directions. The upper one shows horses and their riders, the lower one chariots pulled by horses. The driver in each case is armed with a whip and one passenger rides behind. On the north side (Pl. 170), again, there are two levels: the animals in the upper panel appear to be winged, and the lower panel shows three animals being herded by a rather blurred human figure. These panels together give an idea of life on the road and the farm a thousand years ago.

Left: Pl. 167. Cross of Scriptures: south side, upper panels.
Below: Pl. 168. Cross of Scriptures: south side, under ring arc.

The other two sides of the base may be seen in Pls 154 and 165. The west side (Pl. 154) is much eroded; the upper, less worn panel shows a series of upright figures. The lower panel has vague depictions of animals on its lower section. The south side (Pl. 165) features a row of figures with spears on the upper panel, while the lower shows some animals, possibly deer, running ahead of the hunters.

Pl. 169. Cross of Scriptures: base, east face.

Pl. 170. Cross of Scriptures: base, north side.

South Cross

This is the other of the two complete crosses at Clonmacnoise, and may be slightly earlier than the more decorated Cross of the Scriptures. The South Cross originally stood at the south-west corner of the cathedral, before being moved into the Interpretative Centre. Its place has been taken by a replica. The photographs displayed here were taken of the original in 1989 (unless otherwise designated). The cross is very different in design from the Cross of the Scriptures, being almost completely covered with Celtic decorations of great variety and intricacy. It shows signs of weathering, as the designs were fast disappearing before being moved indoors.

Pl. 171. South Cross: east face with round tower.

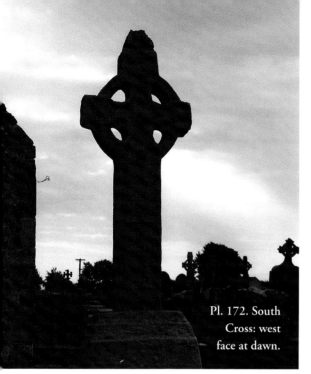

Pl. 172. South Cross: west face at dawn.

Pl. 173. South Cross west face in the afternoon.

East Face

Plate 171 shows the east face of the South Cross with the round tower in the background. The head is rather plain, with five bosses stippled with interlacing. Below, on the shaft, are eight smaller bosses arranged in what appears at first sight to be two groups of five, the middle two belonging in both groups. Below this is a vine scroll, incorporating birds and quadrupeds.

West Face

The west face (Pl. 172) is shown first in silhouette at dawn, and then later at about three o'clock in the afternoon (Pl. 173). The head's west face is similar to its east face. It has on its shaft two faded panels of interlacing, above which a depiction of the crucifixion, with kneeling figures on each side, can just be made out (Pl. 174). Above this are two figures seated back to back. Finally, Plate 175 shows it in the golden light of sunset.

The present appearance of the cross and the state of the graveyard can be contrasted with the lithograph of 1857, included in Henry O'Neill's collection of *Illustrations of The Most Interesting of the Sculptured Crosses of Ancient Ireland* (Fig. 15). Here we can see the decorations of head, shaft and base. The cross is shown surrounded by grave slabs, now housed in the Interpretative Centre. The photograph (Fig. 16) shows contemporary upright gravestones, suggesting that O'Neill made a visual collection of these ancient slabs and grouped them around the base of the South Cross.

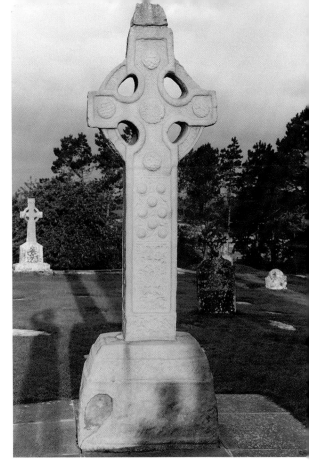

Above left: Pl. 174. South Cross: detail of crucifixion.

Top: Pl. 175. South Cross: west face at sunset.

Left: Fig. 15. O'Neill lithograph of South Cross (Special Collections, Trinity College Dublin).

Above: Fig. 16. 1860s photograph of South Cross.

Pl. 176. South Cross: north side (replica).

North Side
The north side is also covered by panels of interlacing (Pl. 176) on all its aspects.

South Side
The south side shows a sequence of well-defined panels of interlacing, on the shaft, under the ring and at the top (Pls 177 and 178).

North Cross
The final cross at Clonmacnoise is now only a fragment – a shaft with no head and no base. If one wanted an example of a stone carved by time, the North Cross is such an example. The sandstone is deeply pitted, giving a certain ghostly character to the carvings.

131

South Side

The south side is the most notable as it has several panels of spirals above and interlacing below, and is seen in Plate 179 against the small round tower, and in more detail in Plate 180. Its interest lies in the depiction on a lower panel of a seated figure, who gazes directly out at the viewer (Pl. 181). Is it a Sheela-na-gig, that provocative female form found on many old buildings around Ireland? No, this figure sits with legs modestly folded in front, in a Buddha-like pose. It is believed to be a carving of Cernunnos, a horned pagan deity.[8] (Harbison raises both possibilities.)[9]

**Pl. 177. South Cross: shaft,
south side.**

**Pl. 178. South Cross: head,
south side.**

Above: Pl. 179. North Cross: west face
and south side.
Right: Pl. 180. North Cross: south side.

East and West Faces
The east face is uncarved and not shown. The west face has a series of panels filled with interlacing (Pl. 182).

Leaving Clonmacnoise, the route to the next group of high crosses lies to the east, to that famous monastic site at Kells, County Meath, whose lineage goes back to one of the earliest and most celebrated Irish saints, Columba.

Pl. 181. North Cross, seated figure, south side.

Pl. 182. North Cross: upper part of shaft, west face.

1. Rolleston T.W. (tr.), 'The Dead at Clonmacnoise' in W.B. Yeats (ed.), *A Book of Irish Verse* (London: Methuen, 1911), p. 197.

2. Harbison Peter, *Guide to National and Historic Monuments of Ireland* (3rd ed., Dublin: Gill and Macmillan 2001), p. 276.

3. Scherman, Katharine, *The Flowering of Ireland* (London: Little, Brown, 1981) p. 123.

4. Peter Harbison *Pilgrimage in Ireland: The Monuments and the People* (New York: Syracuse University Press, 1991), p. 51.

5. *Ibid.*, p. 115.

6. Harbison, Peter, *The High Crosses of Ireland: An Iconographical and Photographic Survey* (vol. i, Bonn: Dr Rudolf Habelt GMBH, 1992), p. 54.

7. *Ibid.*, p. 49.

8. MacCana, Proinsias, *Celtic Mythology* (London: Hamlin, 1970), p. 44.

9. Harbison 1992 *op. cit.*, p. 53.

CHAPTER 7

KELLS:
THAT ANCIENT SANCTUARY

The modern town of Kells has grown up on the flat land next to a small hill. A thousand years ago a large monastery occupied much of the land now taken over by the town. What remains of the old church buildings is situated on the top of this hill and it is here that some of the most precious of all the high crosses are found. Another significant high cross used to stand at the edge of a narrow street, next to the market. It has now been moved to a safer place, near the entrance to the town.

Kells is an important site for a number of reasons. It became a refuge for the monks of Iona when that community suffered Viking raids. The abbot and his followers managed to flee and founded an inland sanctuary at Kells.[1] It is believed that they brought with them the *Book of Kells*, and perhaps other illuminated texts that have not survived. Certainly, the *Book of Durrow* and the *Book of Lindisfarne* are believed to be associated with the family of monasteries derived from the inspiration of St Columba and his followers.[2] Thus, the importance of this centre of spiritual and artistic life cannot be overestimated. The monastery at Kells is likely to have been the disseminator of much of the iconography – both representational scriptural figures and Celtic decoration – that is to be found on the high crosses in other monastic centres throughout the countryside.

Kells did not avoid its own disasters, however. It was raided many times in the course of the tenth and eleventh centuries, first by Vikings coming from Dublin and then by Irish marauding parties. The Normans then occupied the site. It was broken up at the time of the dissolution of the monasteries and never regained its power. Much of the monastery enclosure has disappeared under the walls and streets of the modern town.

A trip to the top of the hill will take the traveller to the modern churchyard. There is a round tower there, missing its cap but still a commanding monument, about 30 metres in height. The church we see today was rebuilt in about 1750[3] and has a detached square tower, the remains of an older structure. In the churchyard there are three high crosses, all telling the viewer something special about the genre.

Pl. 183. Cross of St Patrick
and St Columba: west face.

Pl. 184. Cross of St Patrick and
St Columba: east face.

Cross of St Patrick and St Columba

The first high cross of note is known as the Cross of St Patrick and St Columba, because an inscription in Latin appears on the upper surface of the base: 'PATRICII ET COLUMBAE CRUX' – or, in English, 'The Cross of St Patrick and St Columba'.

This inscription is not visible when looking straight at the cross. The cross is set dramatically against the base of the round tower (Pls 183 and 194). The various sections of the cross contain both scriptural depictions and interlacing, but there is no attempt to set these off in separate panels. Overall, the cross displays a softness of outline which is most delightful. The cross was included in the collection of lithographs made by Henry O'Neill in 1857. The pictures he drew can be compared with modern photographs (Pls 183 and 184), given in this order to correspond with that set by O'Neill in his 1857 lithograph (Fig. 17).

East Face

The centre of the head on the east face (Pl. 185) has no scriptural figure; instead it is occupied by a pattern of seven bosses. On the left arm is a carving of the sacrifice of Isaac, and St Anthony and St Paul in the desert are depicted on the right. A scene showing two seated figures is difficult to make out at the top of the cross. The ring on both sides has interlacing contained within a roped border. The volutes are centred around the cross rather than on the ring. This is the same position as at Drumcliff, attesting to the association between these crosses.

**Fig. 17. O'Neill lithograph of Cross of St Patrick and St Columba
(Special Collections, Trinity College Dublin).**

Below: Pl. 185. Cross of St Patrick and
St Columba: head, east face.
Right: Pl. 186. Cross of St Patrick and
St Columba: shaft, east face.

Pl. 187. Cross of St Patrick and
St Columba: base, east face.

Pl. 188. Cross of St Patrick and St
Columba: upper shaft and head,
east face.

Pl. 189. Cross of St Patrick
and St Columba: end of
north arm.

Pl. 190. Cross of St Patrick and St Columba: base, north side.

The shaft (Pl. 186) has a set of nine circles of interconnected interlacings. The figures above this must be read from the bottom up if the chronological order is to be followed. At the centre of the shaft is a depiction of Adam and Eve in their nakedness on one side, and Cain slaying Abel on the other. Above this are the three children in the fiery furnace, which is being stoked by two other human figures, and at the top of the shaft is Daniel in the lions' den. Daniel is shown in the narrow segment of the cross head, immediately below the bosses. The base of the cross features a hunting scene (Pl. 187).

West Face
The centre of the head features the figure of Christ in glory (Pls 183 and 188). Christ is flanked by two beasts of uncertain species. Both arms of the cross and the top are occupied by small interlinked bosses. The shaft has just two sections. At the bottom is freely carved interlacing with human figures: their heads are in the corners and their bodies extend into the centre. A band of fretwork demarcates this section both above it and below it. Strangely, the crucifixion is at the top of the shaft, with the two soldiers, one on each side. Two other figures are crowded in above Christ's outstretched arms. Diagonal interlacing covers the rest of the shaft on the west face. The base (just visible in Pl. 191) portrays a procession of horses and riders.

North Side

The shaft of the north side is covered by interlacing, which can be seen in Plate 183. The end of the arm illustrates Daniel slaying a lion (Pl. 189). At the top are carvings of two figures, perhaps St Patrick and St Columba, for whom the cross is named. The base (Pl. 190) features interlacing.

South Side

The south side (Pls 191–3) shows beautiful interlacing, bordered by a series of four birds, two above and two below. The full cross is shown against the ivied church. On the arm is a dramatic carving of Daniel in action against a lion (Pl. 192), in contrast to that seen at the end of the north arm. At the top, the symbol of the evangelist St Mark – the lion – is the only one that can now be identified. Interlacing covers the surface of the south side of the base (Pl. 193).

Pl. Cross of St Patrick and St Columba: south side

Pl. 192. Cross of St Patrick and St Columba: end of arm and top of shaft, south side

The cross can be seen in its surroundings in Plate 194: small in scale compared to the round tower amid the shadows of nearby yew trees.

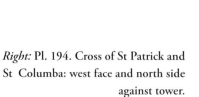

Left: Pl. 193. Cross of St Patrick and St Columba: base, south side.

Right: Pl. 194. Cross of St Patrick and St Columba: west face and north side against tower.

Pl. 195. Unfinished
Cross: east face.

Unfinished Cross

The Unfinished Cross (in fact, it is hardly begun) is an immense structure, over three metres high (Pls 195). It stands beside the church, not very far from the Cross of St Patrick and St Columba. The top appears to be broken off. At the junction of the arms on the east face is the sole finished carving: that of the crucifixion (Pl. 197). The south arm shows three figures, blocked off for more detailed carving later. Four very weathered volutes are attached to the cross in similar fashion to its nearby companion. Panels are raised, apparently waiting for the carver's hand. The circle has already been carved in minutely detailed interlacing. The cross, despite the fact that it is weathered and broken, is a stunning monument when seen against the sunset.

Right: Pl. 196.
Unfinished Cross
against tower.
Below: Pl. 197.
Unfinished Cross:
head, east face,
showing crucifix.

Pl. 198. Broken Cross against round tower.

Broken Cross

The churchyard has more to show. In the graveyard is the broken-off shaft of a further cross (Pl. 198). Harbison suggests that in its unbroken state it must have been one of the most imposing of all Irish high crosses.[4] This is because it shows scenes not found on crosses elsewhere.

East Face

Even in the fragment that remains can be made out a sequence of important events in Christ's life on earth. First, in the lowest panel, is his baptism (Pl. 199). Above this is the wedding feast at Cana. The middle panel displays Christ healing the sick on the left and, on the right, Christ interacting with a woman, as he did at the well at Samaria. Out of sequence, however, on the upper panel, is a depiction of the washing of the child Jesus. The final complete panel is associated with the nativity stories, where the wise men are depicted questioning Herod.

Pl. 199. Broken Cross: east face.

Pl. 200. Broken Cross:
west face, showing
Adam and Eve.

Pl. 201. Broken Cross:
north side.

Pl. 202. Broken Cross: north side, lower panel.

Pl. 203. Broken Cross: north side, upper panel.

West Face

The west face is severely weathered. The lowest panel shows Adam and Eve (Pl. 200) and above that three panels, which are now indecipherable.

North Side

The lowest panel shows interlacing with two human heads placed centrally, separated by four bosses, with further pairs of bosses above and below (Pl. 202). Out of these snakes emerge and spiral up to bite the human heads. The middle panel consists of rather low-relief fretwork merging into a series of bosses. At the top, what first appears to be abstract interlacing of diagonals – both narrow and broad bands – is also ornamented at each corner with animal heads (Pl. 203).

South Side

A series of interlacing and fret designs can be seen (Pl. 204). At the bottom bosses in pairs, large in the centre and small above and below, are separated by a sunken narrow cross. Above this there is a panel of eight spirals of interlacing and over this are multiple bosses arranged in three columns. Next is a panel of diamond-shaped fretwork, each diamond containing a small boss. The top panel, of which the top left-hand corner is missing, consists of eight coils of snakes in elaborate spiral form, linked diagonally.

Pl. 204. Broken Cross: south side.

Market Cross

The street-backed photographs of the Market Cross were taken in 1990, when it stood in the centre of town, in the marketplace. It had lost its top many years previously. It has now been moved to a safer location, at the end of town, with a glass roof over it. The details of the cross were taken mostly at the latter site. Even in the marketplace its positioning was not original – it had been placed there in 1688, according to an inscription on the base. In this central site it had been turned 90 degrees from the standard positioning, making the east face point southwards. Since the marketplace photographs were taken the cross has been moved and reorientated to a more conventional east–west configuration. This configuration will be used to describe all the photographs.

Pl. 205. Market Cross: east face.

Above: Pl. 206. Market Cross: base, east face.
Left: Pl. 207. Market Cross: west face.

153

Above: Pl. 208. Market Cross: base, west face.
Below: Pl. 209. Market Cross: at the crossroads.

Pl. 210. Market Cross: lower shaft, north side.

East Face

The centre of the head (Pl. 205) shows Daniel in the lions' den – a story of extreme danger, but one of rescue this side of death. The arms show differing stories. That on the left shows Abraham prepared to sacrifice Isaac, but delivered by an angel's intervention. On the right, Anthony in the desert is tempted by devils. The ring is covered with very fine interlacing within a border. The volutes are attached to the cross itself, similar in position to those on the Cross of St Patrick and St Columba.

The shaft shows, at the bottom, Christ in the tomb with the soldiers dozing above. Next appears David acclaimed king of Israel by the warriors. The top panel is divided in two, with Adam and Eve on the left and Cain slaying Abel on the right. The base of the Market Cross is full of interest, with a succession of scenes. Its east face shows a progression of horsemen (Pl. 206).

155

Pl. 211. Market Cross: upper part including under arm and end of arm, north side.

West Face

The west face of the head (Pl. 207) shows a crucifixion scene, with the two soldiers present. On each arm of the cross are two figures, said to represent ecclesiastics. The shaft is missing its lowest panel. The middle panel, however, shows Christ blessing the children and the next panel, reading upwards, features the healing of the centurion's servant. At the top panel of the shaft, Christ is shown distributing the loaves and fishes.

The west face of the base (Pl. 208) shows a procession of animals headed by two deer with magnificent antlers. From Plate 209 one gets an idea of the vulnerable position of the Market Cross, placed as it was until recently in the market crossroads.

North Side

These pictures were taken in 2006, after the cross was moved to its new site, away from busy traffic. The lowest panel (Pl. 210) shows two figures wrestling or embracing. It has been variously interpreted as signifying John the Baptist embracing Christ, Judas kissing Christ in the Gethsemane betrayal scene, and even Jacob wrestling with the angel. Above this panel almost half of the stone is missing and the identity of the figure remaining is uncertain. Above this is shown the arrest of Christ.

The top of the cross can be seen in Plate 211. A strange series of figures occupies the topmost panel: a horned central figure has an animal on each side on its hind legs. Harbison[5] cites Ross in suggesting this is Cernunnos, a pagan or Antichrist figure, depicted also in the Clonmacnoise graveyard (Pl. 181, p. 154). In the cross depicted here, the central figure is upright and horned, with a dog on its hind legs on each side. The area underneath the arm of the cross features a series of four squares with interlacing diagonals, flanked by borders of coarser interlacing. On the end of the arm St Paul and St Anthony, holding crossed staffs, are fed by a raven – the small top-central figure.

The north side of the base has a sequence of birds, animals and a centaur (Pl. 212).

South Side

The lowest panel (Pl. 213) shows a stag with a dog on its back – an image more linked to old Irish sagas than to biblical scenes. Above this panel is one from the Old Testament, depicting the judgement of Solomon. The central figure is upside

Pl. 212. Market Cross: base, north side.

Right: Pl. 213. Market Cross: shaft, south side. *Far right:* Pl. 214. Market Cross: under arm and end of arm, south side.

down and soldiers stand on each side. Considerable damage has encroached on this and the next panel, which portrays the story of Samuel anointing David. The interpretation of the topmost panel (Pl. 214) is controversial: it may represent Moses receiving the tablets of the law.

The end of the arm shows Daniel slaying a lion. The base (Pl. 215) shows men with spears and shields facing each other in warlike stance.

Clonmacnoise and Kells together represent two of the three most splendid Irish high-cross groupings that remain despite the weather, neglect, accident and vandalism of the intervening years. The third such grouping, at Monasterboice, is not far from Kells, and close to the first scriptural cross that was highlighted – that at Termonfeckin. The group of high crosses at the ancient monastic site at Monasterboice is remote from the bustle of the city and even from that of the modern parish. It is situated in a graveyard along a winding lane, among green fields, where a total of three entire crosses are to be found. Two of these represent the art of the Irish sculptor before the Norman invasion at its highest point.

Pl. 215. Market Cross: base, south side.

1. Harbison, Peter, *Guide to National and Historic Monuments of Ireland* (3rd ed., Dublin: Gill and Macmillan, 2001), p. 261.
2. Harbison, Peter, *The Golden Age of Irish Art: The Medieval Achievement 600–1200* (London: Thames and Hudson, 1999), pp 26 and 160.
3. Lewis, Samuel, *Atlas Comprising the Counties of Ireland and a General Map of the Kingdom* (London: S. Lewis, 1837).
4. Harbison, Peter, *The High Crosses of Ireland: An Iconographical and Photographic Survey* (vol. i, Bonn: Dr Rudolf Habelt GMBH, 1992), p. 100.
5. *Ibid.*, p. 104, citing Ross, Anne, *Pagan Celtic Britain: Studies in Iconography and Tradition* (London: Routledge, 1967).

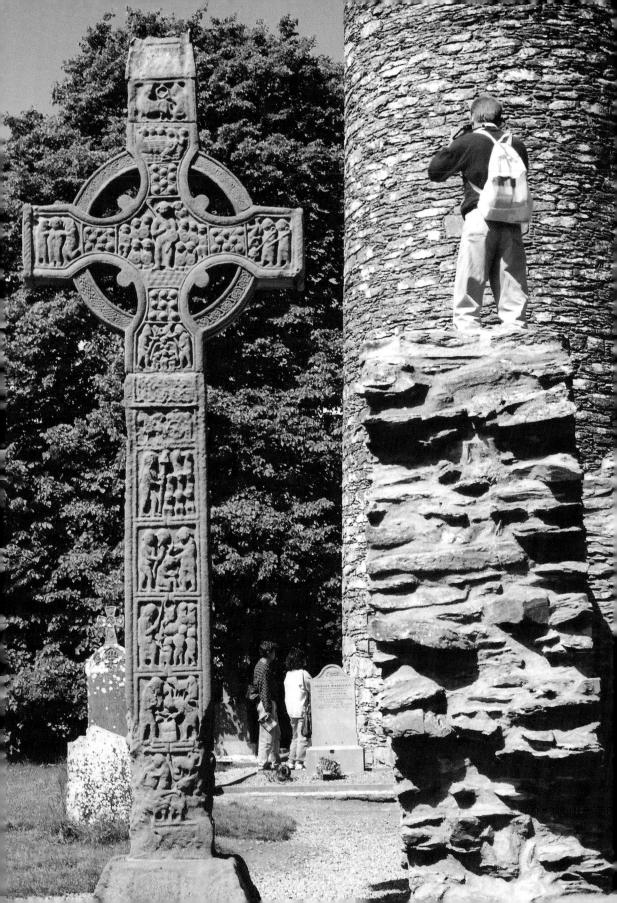

CHAPTER 8

MONASTERBOICE:
A PLACE APART

This monastic site (Pls 216 and 217) was founded in the sixth century by a little-known saint called Buite,[1] and still retains an air of being set apart, despite the tour buses that drive up its twisting narrow lane on a daily basis. Situated not far from Termonfeckin, Monasterboice lies west of the main road leading from Drogheda to Dundalk. Its three high crosses are all made of sandstone and each is quite distinct. They were carved in the tenth century, at a time when there appears to have been a lull in Viking raids (called the '40-year recess'),[2] during which dedicated churchmen rebuilt churches and cathedrals, rescuing them from their earlier state of neglect. The round tower, missing its cap, was burned in 1097 along with the whole monastic library and other treasures.

In addition to the crosses and the tower, the ruins of two church buildings remain: one from the ninth century, and a cathedral built in the thirteenth century.

Pl. 216. Distant view of churchyard.

Pl. 217. Closer view of churchyard.

Cross of Muiredach

The Cross of Muiredach gets its name from an inscription on the bottom of the shaft's west face, which states that Muiredach had the cross erected. It is not known who Muiredach was. Of all the high crosses that remain to this day, this is the most monumental and the best preserved. Its magnificence can be seen from any angle – whether against a backdrop of fields, the round tower, the old cathedral ruins or the evergreen tree. Two oblique views are included here (Pls 218 and 219), which give a sense not only of the cross but also of its immediate surroundings, including the round tower and old church. So well is the monument preserved that we see all the scriptural figures in the round, in realistic representations, as if they had been carved only yesterday. This is due to the hardness of the sandstone of which the cross was made. Other crosses depicting human figures from the Bible have shown evidence of weathering. Would they have looked like the Cross of Muiredach when they were first seen? It is unlikely: this cross at Monasterboice is also remarkable for its proportions and its massiveness – its sheer power.

162

Pl. 218. Cross of Muiredach:
south-east aspect, oblique.

East Face

The east face of the Cross of Muiredach is shown in full (except for the base) in Plate 220. O'Neill's lithograph can be seen in contrast in Figure 18. There has been little or no deterioration over the last 150 years. O'Neill depicted a headstone behind the cross, just where we can see it today, showing that the churchyard was already being used as a graveyard at that time. Many other graves are of more recent date. The rotting tree is now gone.

The head of the cross on this face (Pl. 221) has as its centrepiece Christ in judgement. He carries a cross staff in one hand and a sceptre in the other. To the left is seated a musician playing a harp. The left arm is filled with small figures; all face the centre. On the right, next to the centre, two back-to-back musicians play their wind instruments and, further to the right, there is a sequence of figures with their backs to the central figure. Above the central area a seated figure is accompanied by two winged angels. On the topmost arm are two figures with staffs, perhaps

163

representing St Paul and St Anthony holding bread in the desert, with a bird-like figure in the lower right-hand corner. The top of the cross is carved in the shape of a roof, telling something of the roofing in the tenth century. Below the Christ figure is a scene where St Michael weighs the souls (Pl. 222). A small cross-legged devil lies on his back, attempting to rig the scale in his favour, but St Michael rams a stick in his throat and he is thwarted.

The ring is studded with bosses, both large and small, and the volutes are attached to the cross itself.

Pl. 219. Cross of Muiredach: south-west aspect, oblique.

Pl. 220. Cross of Muiredach: east face.

Fig. 18. O'Neill lithograph of Cross of Muiredach (Special Collections, Trinity College Dublin).

The east face of the shaft contains four panels. On the lowest panel there are the familiar scenes: Adam and Eve are placed to the left of Cain slaying Abel (Pl. 224). In the next panel, reading upwards, David departs from Saul and encounters Goliath (Pl. 223). Jumping back in biblical history, in the next panel Moses strikes water from the rock in the desert for the thirsty Israelites, who wait with beakers at the ready. The topmost panel shows a scene from the New Testament: the wise men of the east come with gifts to present gifts to the holy family. In the junction between the lower arms of the cross St Michael weighing the souls of the dead can again be seen (Pl. 222).

Pl. 221. Cross of
Muiredach: head,
east face.

Pl. 222. Cross of
Muiredach: detail
of east face.

The plinth of the shaft at its lower end shows, in high relief, two cats with tails in the air, fighting each other (Pls 224 and 225). Such whimsical figures are seen on all the aspects of the plinth on this cross, each different from the rest. They are unique to the Cross of Muiredach. Could they have been carved to amuse the children who came with their parents to learn stories from the Bible?

The decoration on the base proper (Pl. 225) on the east face is difficult to make out, being both worn and cracked. It is divided horizontally into two panels. The lower panel is further divided vertically in two. The right panel is filled with interlacing, the left now all but obliterated. The upper panel features two human figures on the right, one kneeling, the other seated. Several animals are carved on the left, of doubtful identification.

West Face

On the west face (Pls 226 and 227) the centre of the head is occupied by the crucifixion. The two soldiers stand at each side, one offering vinegar to ease Christ's suffering, the other thrusting a sword into his side. The spaces where the arms of the cross are narrowed are filled with bosses and at the ends of the arms are two crowd scenes. The northern arm is taken to represent the denial of Peter, while the southern arm appears to represent Christ at the moment of resurrection: he flies heavenward, away from the crowd of soldiers. Two complex panels of bosses and interlacing occupy the space above and below the crucifixion. The topmost panel, under the shingle roof, represents the ascension of Christ into heaven, accompanied by an angel on each side.

The ring on the west face is filled with delicate spiral interlacing. On the shaft (Pl. 228), in the lowest panel, Christ's arrest by two soldiers bearing swords can be seen. Christ has only a reed. In the middle panel the central figure is flanked by two more figures, each carrying a book. This is understood to represent Christ risen. In the top panel Christ is shown again, in the centre. To the figure on his right (Peter) he gives the key of the church, and to the other (Paul) he gives a book.

Pl. 223. Cross of Muiredach: upper panels of shaft, east face.

On the plinth (Pl. 229) are two sitting cats – one with its kitten, the other with a bird. Behind them is an inscription, reading:

OR DO MUIREDACH LAS NDERN(A)D(I) CRO(SSA)
Pray for Muiredach who had the cross erected.[3]

The base (Pl. 230) is much worn on the west face and is in two layers. Below, there are two panels of interlacing. Above, a large crack obscures what appear to be animals and a ring filled with fruit on the left.

Pl. 224. Cross of Muiredach: lower panel and plinth, east face.

Pl. 225. Cross of Muiredach: base, east face.

Left: Pl. 226. Cross of
Muiredach: west face.
Below: Pl. 227. Cross of
Muiredach: head, west face.

Right: Pl. 228. Cross of Muiredach:
shaft, west face.
Below: Pl. 229. Cross of Muiredach:
plinth, west face.
Bottom: Pl. 230. Cross of Muiredach:
base, west face.

Pl. 231. Cross of Muiredach: shaft, north side.

North Side

The shaft is occupied by three panels, one of which is pictured here (Pl. 231). The bottom panel is very similar to the top panel. The middle panel shows a series of six circles and two semicircles (shown), each filled with interlacing, which also extends outside the circles to bind all elements together. In the upper panel there are also six circles, but the interconnection strands in this panel are more dominant and come together to form two parallel cords at the bottom.

The plinth (Pl. 232) shows two seated men facing each other and pulling each other's beards. Under the ring (Pl. 233), the hand of God is superimposed over a circular motif and emerges out of an image of two snakes enclosing three heads on the undersurface of the ring. The end of the arm (Pl. 234) depicts the mocking of Christ. At the top of the head, the two figures holding crossed crooks represent St Paul and St Anthony holding the bread that the raven, seen above, has just given them.

Pl. 232. Cross of Muiredach: plinth, north side.

South Side

The animals on this side of the plinth (Pl. 235) are cat-like creatures, whose backs arch until their heads are close as they look out at the passer-by. (The base itself is severely damaged and is not shown.) The south side of the shaft is made up of three panels (Pls 236 and 237) showing Celtic designs of the very highest quality. The lower panel shows ribbon interweaving, with the major theme consisting of two pairs of diagonals. Each end takes the form of a human head, similar to that at Clonmacnoise (Cross of the Scriptures) but in a much better state of preservation. Even the recessed spirals can be made out. In the middle panel, the design is made up of seven sets of bosses, alternating between two and three in a row, each connecting with the next by spiral threads. The top panel is perhaps the *pièce de résistance*, showing two pairs of lambs frolicking among the branches of the tree of life, with birds and grapes within the branches. These are spirals, springing off a central stem.

Under the ring (Pl. 237), between borders of interlacing, are two snakes looping around three heads. One has its head at the top; the other has its head at the bottom. Under the arm of the cross two animals lie side by side with their legs facing each other. At the very end of the south arm (Pl. 238) Pilate washes his hands. On the top, just below the gable end, a horseman rides.

Above left: Pl. 233. Cross of Muiredach: under arm, north side.
Above and left: Pl. 234. Cross of Muiredach: top and end of arm, north side.

Above: Pl. 235. Cross of Muiredach: lower
panel and plinth, south side.
Above right and right: Pl. 236. Cross of
Muiredach: upper panels of shaft, south side.

Tall Cross

While the Cross of Muiredach in all its solidity compares with the dimensions of the
Ossory crosses, the Tall Cross at Monasterboice, true to its name, is three times as
tall as it is wide and exceeds all other high crosses in height. It stands at 6.45 metres
high and 2.13 metres across the span of its arms (Pl. 239), and provides a striking
contrast to the smooth curve of the round tower. Viewing the cross from the east face
(Pls 240 and 241), the ring appears relatively small in proportion to the shaft, meeting
the arms at the inner slope of their scalloped parts. The volutes are attached to the
cross itself. Because of the cross's height more panels can be fitted in than on the
Cross of Muiredach and the other scriptural crosses at Durrow and Clonmacnoise.
The panels do show more evidence of weathering, however, especially on the shaft.

Left: Pl. 237. Cross of Muiredach: under arm, south side.
Below left: Pl. 238. Cross of Muiredach, end of arm and top, south side.
Below: Pl. 239. Tall Cross: east face with round tower.

Pl. 240. Tall Cross: east face
with photographer.

East Face

In the centre of the head (Pls 240 and 241) Christ is seen in glory, holding both sword and shield and accompanied by soldiers on each side. The narrow parts of the arms are covered by bosses, eight above and on each side; in the space below the central figure there are nine bosses. On the arms are two post-biblical scenes relating to St Anthony and St Paul in the desert and the temptation of St Anthony. Above the central set of bosses (Pl. 241) a boat filled with apostles is seen in the background to Christ walking on water. The topmost panel shows an animal and a human figure, the interpretation of which is not clear. The roof is gabled and shingled. The ring has deep moulding and is filled with a variety of delicate interlacing. The volutes are attached to the cross, similarly to those on the Cross of Muiredach.

Devoted to stories from the Old Testament, the shaft on the east face (Pl. 242) shows many scenes which are familiar because they have occurred so often on other crosses, as well as some unusual ones. The stories are not in sequence, for the earlier scenes of Isaac's near sacrifice and Moses striking the rock for water come between David slaying a lion (on the bottom panel) and his encounter with Goliath. Reading from the bottom up, the panel of David slaying the lion is considerably damaged (Pl. 240). The sacrifice of Isaac in the next panel is all too vividly complete, with

Above left: Pl. 241. Tall Cross: head, east face.
Above: Pl. 242. Tall Cross: shaft, east face.
Left: Pl. 243. Tall Cross: Tall Cross, west face with North Cross in distance.

Isaac and his bundle of sticks, Abraham with his sword and the rescuing angel with the ram as alternative sacrifice. Next in sequence is Moses striking the rock. An Israelite is shown ready to catch the water and two rows of soldiers wait in line. Above this the sculpture manages to compress two stories into one panel. On the left David holds the head of Goliath, whom he has just slain, and to the right David is anointed by Samuel. In the next panel an unclothed Sampson tilts a narrow column, ready to bring it down on the heads of eight Philistines. Above, a short panel displays a chariot, and the accompanying figures show Elijah ascending to heaven. Next, reading upward, a small slightly raised plinth marks the joint between two separate stones.

The base of the Tall Cross is plain; the shallow plinth does show traces of interlacing but these have been almost totally obliterated by time and weathering.

Above: Pl. 244. Tall Cross: head, west face.
Right: Pl. 245. Tall Cross: shaft, west face.

West Face

In the centre of the head on the west face (Pls 243–5) is a portrayal of the crucifixion. Here Christ's head is at an angle, indicating that he is already dead. The two soldiers are crouched into the concave arc of the cross's arms. On the panel immediately below this are two soldiers raising sticks or lances towards Christ's feet, the meaning of which is uncertain. On each side, in the small space created by the constriction of the arms, two seated figures hold animals. On the edges of the arms we see the mocking of Christ on the left and Judas's kiss in the garden of Gethsemane on the right. Above the crucifixion Peter is depicted drawing his sword to cut off the ear of Malthus. At the top, a seated figure represents Pilate washing his hands as he declares Christ to be innocent. The ring is decorated with triplets of bosses, interspersed with tiny knots of interlacing.

Pl. 246. Tall Cross: shaft, south side.

Above: Pl. 247. Tall Cross: top of shaft
and end of arm, south side.
Above right: Pl. 248. Tall Cross: north
side through break in church wall.
Right: Pl. 249. Tall Cross: under arm,
north side.

Reading from the bottom up, the lowest panel of the shaft on the west face is somewhat damaged, but clearly shows Christ in the tomb. The soldiers adopt the napping posture also depicted on the Cross of the Scriptures at Clonmacnoise. Above this is the baptism of Christ by John the Baptist in the River Jordan. Above this is a triad of panels, each containing three figures. The lowest shows the three holy women at the tomb, bringing spices. Above them the central figure is Christ, handing the keys to St Peter and a book to St Paul. The upper panel shows the raised Christ, similar to that on the west face of the Cross of Muiredach. It is quite damaged.

South Side
This side (Pl. 246) has evidently seen the worst of a millennium of weather. The lowest panel is indecipherable and is not shown. Next is a panel of interlacing around five bosses. The single mid-panel of figures is also much eroded, but is believed to show Elizabeth, Zacharias and the infant John the Baptist.[4] Above is an interlaced pattern similar to that on the lower pane of the south side of the Cross of Muiredach. The next panel shows the naming of John. The area under the ring is too badly weathered to be deciphered. Above the plinth is a winged animal. The underside of the ring shows two bands of interlacing (Pl. 247). The end of the arm is slightly raised in pyramidal form, containing a low-relief key pattern.

North Side
The north side (Pls 248 and 249) cannot be reached by the sun as it is obscured by the adjacent church wall. It is viewed through the broken window space of the church and is somewhat dark. The lowest panel is not illustrated. It is quite damaged. Above this is a panel showing David crowned as king. Above this, in turn, is a set of seven bosses connected with interlacing. In the middle of the shaft Daniel is accosted by two flanking lions. Above this are more panels of interlacing, quite worn. In contrast (Pl. 249), a beam of the early morning sun lights up the clarity of the panel immediately under the arm: a winged four-legged beast turning its head. The carving on the underside of the ring consists of rope designs coiled to form a border, with a central diamond-shaped motif containing interlacing.

North Cross
In contrast with its two companions, the North Cross is largely undecorated. It stands just inside the perimeter of the enclosing wall (Pl. 243). It is made up of three pieces: the head with the upper part of its shaft, the lower shaft and an intervening modern block connecting them.

Pl. 250. North Cross: east face.

East Face
The east face (Pl. 250) shows a slightly raised wide boss decorated with C-scrolls.

West Face
The west face (Pl. 251) shows the crucifixion and the two soldiers, one on each side.

With the beginning of the eleventh century, these highly ornamental high crosses ceased to be erected. The old monastic centres appear to have lost their mandate, to have succumbed to the raids from both foreigners and native warlords and to have become somewhat decadent. A new order of Christian practice came into being in the twelfth century. This was the development of monasteries under Cistercian and Augustinian orders, where uniformity throughout the order, discipline, attention to devotions, liturgy and obedience ruled the monks' lives. In this system, figurative art was not to be encouraged. With the division of the country into more formal dioceses, each with its own bishop, the small Celtic churches came to be replaced by larger cathedrals, built in the imported Romanesque style.

Pl. 251. North Cross: west face.

It seems that for a hundred years, few if any free-standing crosses were erected. When the twelfth century dawned, a new style of high cross was to be found. Some of these new crosses, serving as examples, will be addressed in the final chapter of this book.

1. Harbison, Peter, *Guide to National and Historic Monuments of Ireland* (3rd ed., Dublin: Gill and Macmillan, 2001), p. 238.
2. Henry, Françoise, *Irish Art during the Viking Invasion 800–1020 AD* (London: Methuen, 1967), p. 156.
3. Harbison, Peter, *The High Crosses of Ireland: An Iconographical and Photographic Survey* (vol. i, Bonn: Dr Rudolf Habelt GMBH, 1992), p. 143.
4. *Ibid.*, p. 149.

Chapter 9

Examples of Twelfth-Century High Crosses: Emblems of Diocese

Since the magnificence of Monasterboice, two centuries elapsed before any more crosses were erected. These were different in several ways from the earlier scriptural monuments. Not only had they changed in shape, but they also no longer portrayed the Bible stories which were so characteristic of the ninth- and tenth-century crosses. They did retain depiction of the crucifixion, however, along with one or more ecclesiastical figures. These figures represented either a founding saint or a contemporary bishop. The Celtic design continued, but changed: it was diverted toward a more flowing overall configuration or to a more formally geometric composition. The ring was retained on some of the crosses of this period, sometimes solid with the rest of the head and at other times separated, retaining the volutes of an earlier period.

In the intervening centuries Irish church life had changed quite profoundly. The prosperity of the old monasteries, which had enabled them to foster art and learning, had been turned towards their aggrandisement and secularisation. Aesthetic ideals and discipline had been forgotten, as had pastoral care, confession and preaching.[1] Each monastery was independent of any other and competition between them had sometimes developed into outright war. Monastery leaders, such as those in charge at Clonmacnoise and Durrow, had come to blows and fought each other.[2] Many of the monasteries had come under lay control. The few bishops scattered throughout the country had no formal bishoprics and little power. It was time for a new reform movement, ordered from the head of the western church, the Pope in Rome.[3] Gregory VII brought together a series of synods in Ireland. Over the following years these synods laid the groundwork for the setting up of dioceses throughout the country, under the control of Rome and in conformity with those in England and the rest of Christian Europe. These bishoprics stood in contrast to the monasteries and were designed to provide parishes and priests for the needs of lay communities.

About the same time, new monastic sites under the auspices of the Augustinians and Cistercians were established. These orders brought in homogenous systems of monastic life that stressed poverty, chastity and obedience. Days were divided between prayer and manual labour; the monks were required to survive on what their lands could provide. Larger stone churches were built, contained within the monastery walls. This monastic life appealed to many of the dispirited monks of Celtic monasteries, who then transferred to the new order. Thus Monasterboice and Kells declined, while Mellifont, a Cistercian centre a few miles away, prospered.[4]

Viking raids at this time had increased and the raiders ventured further inland. Monasteries had been pillaged and burned, monks slaughtered and reliquaries looted. These incursions were stopped in the eleventh century by the victory of Brian Boru, but the old Irish monasteries had by then lost much of their energy and were impoverished and disorganised.

Pl. 252. Kilfenora: Doorty's Cross, outside church, west face (1989 photograph).

Pl. 253. Kilfenora: Doorty's Cross, inside church walls, west face (2006 photograph).

The crosses of the twelfth century are products of the progression in church organisation towards a diocesan model, governed by bishops under direct control of the Vatican. Kilfenora in County Clare was, in the twelfth century, a newly formed small diocese. It is said that the cross there was erected to confirm the authority of Rome over the old Irish monastic regime. Dysert O'Dea, in the same county, is in the territory of the reforming King Muirchertach O'Brien. According to Peter Harbison, the decoration of the crosses connected the new reforms with the old traditions, showing decorative interlacing and other abstract art as well as continuing to depict the crucifix.

Right: Pl. 254. Kilfenora: Doorty's
Cross, in church, east face.

Rather than a full coverage of twelfth-century crosses, many of which have been
re-erected from fragments found in their vicinity, this book will present the crosses
at just two sites, about 12 kilometres apart: Kilfenora and Dysert O'Dea. They are
both in County Clare, on the edge of that strange expanse of naked limestone,
stripped bare by glaciers in the Ice Age, known as the Burren. The crosses are made
not from sandstone or granite but from limestone, the like of which can clearly be
seen underlying the West Cross at Kilfenora.

KILFENORA, COUNTY CLARE

The site at Kilfenora originally had seven crosses. Two have been moved offsite. Of those that remain, two are fragmentary and another has little in the way of ornamentation; only the two decorated crosses are included in this collection. Doorty's Cross, the more ornate, used to be sited to the immediate west of the cathedral, where the photograph, Plate 252, was taken in 1989. Recently it was moved inside the cathedral walls and covered with a glass roof (Pl. 253). All the other photographs were taken of the cross in this new position.

Doorty's Cross

This cross (Pls 252–4) is named for a family who used part of it as a tombstone until it was rescued and re-erected. The head has been reattached to the shaft. The cross does have a ring but the arc is not hollowed out from the head. This cross is like no other. Differences include subject matter as well as the form of the sculpture. Some of the details shown on the cross are clear but the meaning of others is obscure. One thing is unmistakable: a bishop, whether depicting founding father or contemporary ecclesiastic, now got pride of place, back to back with the crucifix. On one face of the cross (the west) the carving is flat, while on the other (the east) it is rounded. It is as if each side was carved by a different mason, representing different artistic styles.

West Face

On the west face (Pls 252 and 253), the centre of the head is occupied by a crucifix surrounded by four birds, above and below the arms. It is much worn and there is a break in continuity with the rest of the shaft. However, the detail on the opposite face shows continuity across the crack, so it is likely that the head and shaft belong together. Interlacing in the shape of a figure of eight occupies the top of the shaft section and this leads into two wide ribbons covered with interlacing. At the bottom a man and horse can be seen in profile. This depicts Christ's entry into Jerusalem. The ribbons trace the difficult route Jesus faced during his trial. At the base is a shingled plaque similar to the roof of some earlier high crosses.

Pl. 256. Kilfenora: West Cross, east face.

East Face

On the east face (Pl. 254) a bishop with crozier occupies the head and upper part of the shaft. Two figures representing the desert fathers, St Paul and St Anthony, stand side by side immediately below. Each holds a crozier of a different shape. These figures stand above a strange winged beast trampling on two human heads. What could this mean? It is suggestive of some apocalyptic scene, perhaps where the bishop and his priests have been granted authority to kill the beast, who has humanity in its thrall. The message appears directed at the role of clergy in the cure of souls.

North and South Sides

The north side is covered with interlacing. The south side shows two human figures of unknown significance.

Pl. 257. Kilfenora: West Cross, west face, showing limestone bedrock.

Pl. 258. Kilfenora: West
Cross, head and upper
shaft, west face.

West Cross

The West Cross (Pls 255–9) is very different from Doorty's Cross. Its austere lines
and formal decorations appear to have been drawn with set square, protractor and
ruler. In regard to the carving of figures, only the crucifixion is retained, along with
a small animal inserted at the top of the cross, which appears incongruous with the
rest. It stands in a field adjacent to Doorty's Cross, above the limestone bedrock of
which it is made. It is very well preserved, with low-relief formal fretwork interlacing
in small sections on both the east and west faces. The ring, with volutes attached to
it, is carved free of the scalloped arms of the cross. The edges of the cross, defined
by a narrow border, are straight.

East Face

This shows the crucifix with the Christ figure, fully clothed, occupying the centre of
the head (Pls 255 and 256). A strange beast occupies the top of the cross, above the
crucifix. The rest of the head, including the frontal aspects of the ring, are covered

in tight interlacing. A double-rope moulding extends vertically from a small ledge on which Christ is standing, widening at the bottom to frame a triangular motif, the details of which are not visible. It has been suggested that a shrine may have been attached to this section.[6] The rope moulding separates the two sides of the face, each decorated with different patterns of interlacing.

West Face

The west face (Pls 257–60) is covered entirely by abstract designs. A low-relief motif occupies the centre, criss-crossed by four diagonals. Bold interlacing occupies the head and both arms. The upper shaft is covered by low-relief interlacing, both circular and diagonal. At the bottom, an inverted triangle is covered with interlacing. The limestone bedrock lies just inches below the ground surface (Pl. 257).

DYSERT O'DEA, COUNTY CLARE

This site lies just 12 kilometres from Kilfenora. It is on the site of an early Christian monastery, founded by St Tola in the eighth century. The name of the cross is explained on the base by an inscription, which relates how it was repaired and re-erected in the seventeenth century by Conor O'Dea.[5]

The twelfth-century cross (Pls 260–62) stands in a field opposite a Romanesque church. Its small pyramidal top is modern and it is placed upon a modern base. There is no ring, but volutes jut out from the edges of the cross's arms. The head, shaft and upper base are all separate fragments, which may or may not belong together.

Pl. 259 Kilfenora: West Cross, triangle on lower shaft, west face.

Pl. 260. Dysert O'Dea: cross in field near Romanesque church.

East Face

The head of the cross depicts a crucifixion, and below it on the shaft there is the figure of a bishop with crozier (Pl. 261). A strange hole can be seen on the bishop's arm, which may have been his other arm protruding to hold a reliquary, as suggested by Peter Harbison.[7] Interlacing covers the pyramidal base, except where it has been cut away to allow an inscription to document the repair of the cross by a member of the O'Dea family in 1683.

West Face

The west face is entirely covered by abstract geometric art designs (Pl. 262). The head is taken up by a decoration of five lozenges in the form of a St Brigid's cross in high relief. The shaft is divided into a series of sections. The top shows a number of raised squares, the middle four forming a cross. Below this are two separate panels, one square and the other narrow, filled with animal-headed interlacing. The largest panel has a set of diagonals low on the shaft; the space between these is occupied by diamond shapes, which outline tiny crosses. Below this is a narrow band of animal interlacing.

Pl. 261. Dysert O'Dea: east face.

North and South Sides
The north and south sides are covered by panels of interlacing.

Despite the fluid interlacing in the central panel, the Dysert O'Dea cross projects a very limited, rigid, rectilinear appearance, at variance with the sense of flow emanating from the earlier crosses. The message conveyed here appears to be that under the image of Christ crucified the bishop is in charge, and other aspects of the Christian faith may be learned from him and his clergy.

It was in the twelfth century that the Normans invaded Ireland and the whole political and administrative system began to change. It seems, however, that the inspiration and energy that had driven the creation of the high crosses had already faded. Enough remains of the previous golden age, however, not only in the stone high crosses but also in the books and reliquaries stored carefully in our museums, for us to revere and find delight and fresh inspiration for our own day.

Pl. 262. Dysert O'Dea: west face.

1. Stalley, Roger, *The Cistercian Monasteries of Ireland* (New Haven and London: Yale University Press, 1987), p. 11.

2. Harbison, Peter, *The Golden Age of Irish Art: The Medieval Achievement 600–1200* (London: Thames and Hudson, 1999), p. 68.

3. Harbison, Peter, 'Irish Art in the Twelfth Century' in Colum Hourihane (ed.), *From Ireland Coming: Irish Art from the Early Christian to the Late Gothic Period in its European Context* (Princeton University Press, 2001), p. 111.

4. Stalley *op. cit.*, p. 14.

5. Harbison, Peter, *Pilgrimage in Ireland: The Monuments and the People* (New York: Syracuse University Press, 1991), p. 167, citing O'Farrell, Fergus.

6. Harbison, Peter, *The High Crosses of Ireland: An Iconographical and Photographic Survey* (vol. i, Bonn: Dr Rudolf Habelt GMBH, 1992), p. 83.

7. Harbison 1999 *op. cit.*, p. 108.

BIBLIOGRAPHY

Department of the Environment of Northern Ireland, *Historic Monuments of Northern Ireland* (Belfast, 1983).

Ellis, Peter Beresford, *The Celtic Empire* (London: Robinson, 2001).

Harbison, Peter, *Guide to the National Monuments of the Republic of Ireland* (1st ed., Dublin: Gill and Macmillan, 1970).

—, *Pilgrimage in Ireland: The Monuments and the People* (New York: Syracuse University Press, 1991).

—, *The High Crosses of Ireland: an Iconographical and Photographic Survey* (vols i–iii, Bonn: Dr Rudolf Habelt GMBH, 1992).

—, *The Golden Age of Ireland Art: The Medieval Achievement 600–1200* (London: Thames and Hudson, 1999).

—, *Guide to National and Historic Monuments of Ireland* (3rd ed., Dublin: Gill and Macmillan, 2001).

Henry, Françoise, *Irish Art during the Viking Invasion 800–1020* (London: Methuen, 1967).

Hourihane, Colum, *From Ireland Coming: Irish Art from the Early Christian to the Late Gothic Period in its European Context* (Princeton University Press, 2001).

Hughes, Kathleen, *Irish High Crosses* (Dublin: Three Candles Press, 1964).

—, *The Church in Early Irish Society* (Ithaca: Cornell University Press, 1966).

— and Hamlin, Ann, *Celtic Monasticism: the Modern Traveller to the Early Irish Church* (New York: Seabury Press, 1981).

Leask, Harold G., *Irish Churches and Monastic Buildings* (vol. i, Dundalk: Dundalgan Press, 1955).

McGrath, Fergal, *Education in Ancient and Medieval Ireland* (Dublin: Skellig Press, 1951).

O'Neill, Henry, *Illustrations of the Most Interesting of the Sculptured Crosses of Ireland* (London: Trübner, 1857).

Porter, A. Kingsley, *The Crosses and Culture of Ireland* (New York: Benjamin Blom, 1930).

Richardson, Hilary and Scarry, John, *An Introduction to Irish High Crosses* (Dublin: Mercier Press, 1990).

Roe, Helen M., *High Crosses of Western Ossory* (Kilkenny: Kilkenny Archeological and Historical Society, 1969).

—, *High Crosses of Kells* (Navan: Meath Archeological and Historical Society, 1981).

—, *Monasterboice and its Monuments* (Dundalk: Louth Archaeological and Historical Society, 1981).

Ryan, Michael, *Ireland and Insular Art* (Dublin: Royal Irish Academy, 1987).

Rynne, Etienne (ed.), *Figures from the Past* (Dublin: Glendale Press, 1981).

Scherman, Katharine, *The Flowering of Ireland* (London: Little, Brown, 1981).

School of Environmental Studies, Trinity College, Dublin, *The Heritage of Clonmacnoise* (Trinity College, Dublin, 1987).

Seaborne, Malcolm, *Celtic Crosses of Britain and Ireland* (Princes Risborough: Shire Archaeology, 1989).